D0848495

# C. H. GUENTHER & SON AT 150 YEARS

## THE LEGACY OF A TEXAS MILLING PIONEER

# C·H·GUENTHER & SON

## AT 150 YEARS

# The Legacy of a
# Texas Milling Pioneer

## LEWIS F. FISHER

Ⓜ

Maverick Publishing Company

Copyright © 2001 by C. H. Guenther & Son, Inc.

MAVERICK PUBLISHING COMPANY
P.O. Box 6355, San Antonio, Texas 78209

All rights reserved. No portion of this book may be reproduced in any form
or by any means, including electronic storage and retrieval systems, without
explicit, written permission of the publisher, except for brief passages
excerpted for review and critical purposes.

ALSO BY LEWIS F. FISHER

*Saving San Antonio: The Precarious Preservation of a Heritage*
*Crown Jewel of Texas: The Story of San Antonio's River*
*San Antonio: Outpost of Empires*
*The Spanish Missions of San Antonio*

Library of Congress Cataloging-in-Publication Data

Fisher, Lewis F.
    C.H. Guenther & Son at 150 years : the legacy of a Texas milling
        pioneer / Lewis F. Fisher.
            p.     cm.
    Includes bibliographical references and index.
    ISBN 1-893271-14-5 (alk. paper).
        1. Flour mills—Texas—History. 2. C.H. Guenther & Son Inc.—
    History. 3. Flour industry—Texas—History. 4. Texas—History.
    I. Title.
    TS2135.U6 .T4 2000
    338.7'66472'009764—dc21                          00-048027

07 06 05 04 03 02 01 00 99 98      5 4 3 2 1

Printed in the United States of America

*Frontispiece:* This frame mill on a small peninsula formed by the San Antonio
River remained the main building of Guenther's San Antonio operation from
its construction in 1878 until it was replaced in 1914.

# Contents

# Introduction

Quality Food Products Since 1851

At the milestone of 150 years, C. H. Guenther & Son, Inc. shows few signs of advanced age, other than the beard on the founder's picture on Pioneer brand products and the ancient mementos spread through his old home beside the mill in San Antonio, Texas, and in the foyer of corporate headquarters next door.

Today's C. H. Guenther & Son executives have no flowing beards. They fly in jet planes to distant subsidiaries and talk of product development, brand recognition and strategic plans. The loud splash of water forcing creaking machinery to turn stones that spit out ground grain gave way long ago to the hum of rows of automated machines transforming grain from raw kernels into packaged products without the touch of human hands. Even the original focus on milling has been tempered with production of increasingly popular prepackaged frozen foods.

Yet tradition, if not always obvious, is sensed deeply at the company, quite aware that it has become, so far as is known, not only the oldest family-owned business in Texas but also the oldest milling company continuously owned by the same family in the nation.

When Carl Hilmar Guenther (the name is still pronounced GEN-thur) left his native Saxony at the age of 22 to cross the ocean in search of opportunity, he ended up living the American dream. He spent time in several areas of the United States before arriving in Texas in 1851, then eight years later refined his choice for a permanent milling operation from the German community of Fredericksburg to the larger town of San Antonio. There he prospered. By the time of his death in 1902, Guenther could see that the company he built on the Texas frontier had a good chance of continuing successfully through the next generation, and even beyond. As, indeed, the company has.

This is its story.

Guenther-haus, Pfeffergasse
Conrad Lucke                    WEISSENFELS.

Carl Hilmar Guenther grew to adulthood in this home
in Wiessenfels, a prosperous German town some
20 miles west of Leipzig.

# 1. Journey to Texas

This portrait of Carl Hilmar Guenther was made in Germany prior to his departure for America in 1848, when he was 22.

Texas was brimming with opportunity when, at the age of 24, Carl Hilmar Guenther arrived to seek his fortune.

"Texas is now the place where you can make money," he wrote home to Germany after a grueling walk beside a wagon train from the Gulf Coast brought him to San Antonio in January 1851. "Living here is not as pleasant as living in Germany or other parts of the States," he allowed, but, beyond the coastal plains, "it is as healthy as it is where you live, you can tell that by the healthy color and complexion of the local people."

The end of the Mexican War scarcely three years earlier had settled the question of who owned Texas. Now European immigrants were flooding into the young state, creating a kaleidoscopic jumble of races, languages and townscapes that enchanted travelers and bespoke the American dream.

Guenther brought with him attitudes and skills needed in the new land. Born in the Prussian province of Saxony, southwest of Leipzig near Weissenfels, to a well-to-do family of cloth merchants and Lutheran clergymen known for championing the cause of peasants, he was the third of eight children and the eldest son of Carl Gottfried and Johanna Rosina Koerner Guenther. He was schooled by private tutors and then apprenticed to a miller. At the age of 18 he was accepted into the guild of master millwrights in Sachsen.

An earnest youth of medium height, with a steady gaze, straight dark hair combed across a high forehead and a broad moustache that spilled into a full beard in his later years, Carl Hilmar Guenther developed the requisite physical strength and ingenuity, and with it mental alertness, while learning the miller's trade. His empirical bent was evident as a boy in Saxony when he got his first pair of glasses. To test the spectacles, he walked out of the store to

Guenther completed his Piano School book at the age of 10 when the family was living on its Wiedebach estate near Weissenfels. The notes are some of those he drew for a schottische ("Scottish") dance, similar to the polka but with a slower tempo.

the church next door, climbed the steeple and was "overjoyed" at the distances he could see.

Naturally restless and now increasingly independent, he chafed under time-worn strictures for advancement. Though well tutored in literary classics and other basics of the time, and with good technical training as well, he felt frustrated in trying to broaden his education in drawing, in particular, which his father apparently thought impractical. He lamented the political rigidity of provincial princes. Nor did he relish the traditional idea of an arranged marriage that his parents seemed to favor.

So Carl Hilmar Guenther set out to see the world.

Giving up thoughts of going to France or Russia in favor of checking out reports on America, he quietly quit his job at a mill in nearby Zeitz, borrowed money from a friend, took the train up to the North Sea coast and, at 2 p.m. on May 5, 1848, left Bremerhaven aboard the *Leibnitz* for New York.

His parents—who had kept telling him, "Stay in your own country and learn to make an honest living here"— were among the last to know.

"I knew that Father would not be in sympathy with my ideas," he explained in a letter he sent as he was leaving Zeitz. He hoped his parents would not see his decision as "a silly prank, for I have had this in mind for a long time and have considered it from every angle." After he docked in New York he elaborated: "As soon as I would leave our own home and make little trips around the country to acquaint myself with conditions in Germany, I found that nothing appealed to me. Business and life in general seemed dead. The streets were narrow and dull. In fact, I felt hemmed in. Not until I made my final decision to leave did I ever feel joy or peace."

America, likewise, was carefully checked out after he arrived. Deciding against staying in New York City, Guenther and a companion took a steamer up the Hudson River to Albany and then a horse-drawn boat westward on the Erie Canal. "This was slow traveling," he recalled, "but as the weather was fine and the scenery lovely, I regarded it as a pleasure trip, even though the meals and living conditions on the boat were bad. Everywhere we were asked by the farmers to get off and help with the farmwork, as they were harvesting."

Tempted to stop, but with a letter of introduction from Zeitz to an acquaintance in Wisconsin, Guenther con-

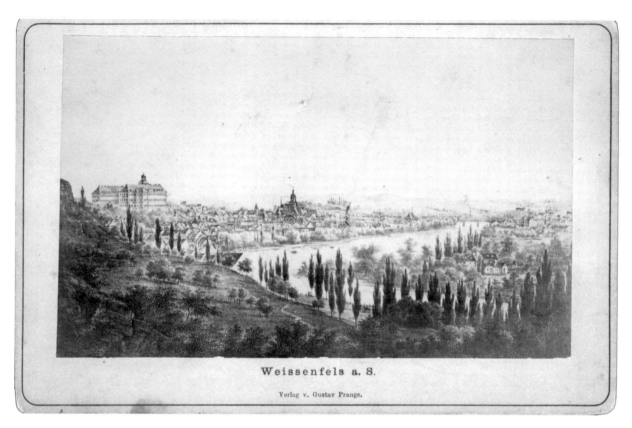

Weissenfels a. S.

Verlag v. Gustav Prange.

Carl Hilmar Guenther grew to adulthood in Wiessenfels, a county seat town on the Saale River in the province of Saxony, some 20 miles west of Leipzig.

tinued on to Buffalo and stepped immediately onto a steamer for the four-day voyage on Lakes Erie, Huron and Michigan to Racine, Wisconsin, home to 3,000 people, nearly half of them foreign-born and a third of those of German origin. Lumber and grain products shipped out by its sizable milling industry helped make Racine a larger port at the time than Milwaukee, 20 miles up the lake to the north.

"This little town had an extraordinary attraction for me," Guenther later wrote. For nearly two years he worked in and around Racine—with stays in nearby Michigan and Ohio sandwiched in—as a farmhand, at a sawmill, at a steam-powered gristmill, at a harvesting machinery factory and as a carpenter. Walking in the countryside, he found refuge one snowy night with five Indians in a deerskin hut. ("The Indian is very amiable, but once he is aroused he is worse than a bear or a lion," he wrote.)

Although otherwise usually in the company of fellow German immigrants, he took the opportunity during some winter months to take lessons in English: "In these classes there were children of eight and men of thirty, all reading the same lessons."

For nearly two years Carl Hilmar Guenther based himself in Racine, Wisconsin, where he felt comfortable with the sizable German population and a milling industry that made Racine a larger Great Lakes port than nearby Milwaukee.

Back home, Guenther's father turned out to be more tolerant of his son's wanderings than expected.

"You did not ask my permission to go to America, so I cannot advise you to come back," his father wrote. "I leave the decision entirely to your own judgement. . . . If I see that you are serious, then I will stand by you and, if your plans are reasonable, I will help you to the best of my ability."

Carl Hilmar Guenther, usually called just Hilmar to distinguish him from his father, felt sufficiently encouraged to broach the subject of his inheritance. There was an opportunity—if he had $2,000—to go into the lumbering business in Wisconsin. This would be a fine time, he suggested, to receive his inheritance; after all, his oldest sister, Amanda, received her $2,000 inheritance at a young age, when she married.

"It would be a good thing for you if part of your estate were invested here in America," the son added, "for I could do much better business here in America than in Germany."

Rather than pursue lumbering, he agreed to return home for a visit, but only after he had seen the southern part of the United States. Hard as it was to leave the gala German social life of Racine, with its dances, singing societies and shooting galleries, in October 1850 he took a steamer down Lake Michigan to Chicago, crossed Illinois by canal and boarded a Mississippi steamboat for an adventure-filled trip to St. Louis and then down to Lake

*"I wrote from New Orleans that soon I might write home for money," Guenther informed his father from San Antonio in 1851. "That time has now arrived, for I want to buy land along some river . . . and there build a mill."*

Providence, Louisiana, where he worked in plantation country for two months as a carpenter and cabinetmaker for German immigrants. He wrote home that he would leave New Orleans in the spring and be back in Weissenfels by July.

Instead, two months later he was in New Orleans, ready to depart for Texas.

The attraction seems to have been his discovery that, in Texas, milling talents were in short supply. In San Antonio he was offered $4 a day plus the assistance of three workmen and three pairs of oxen with wagons to build a mill in the countryside. That was far more than he had been offered to be a farmhand in New York (75 cents a day) or earned as a carpenter in Wisconsin ($1.25), a cabinetmaker in Louisiana ($2.50) or a miller in Sheboygan, Michigan ($3).

But thanks to a faraway father sufficiently indulgent to begin doling out his departed son's inheritance, Hilmar Guenther could leap ahead of the pack.

"I wrote from New Orleans that soon I might write home for money," Guenther informed his father from San Antonio in early January 1851. "That time has now arrived, for I want to buy land along some river near here as soon as possible and there build a mill. . . .

"It would be best for you to send the money from Europe as soon as possible," he went on, explaining away his boldness by adding, "If I wait until you offer me the $2,000 it would take another year before I could get the money here."

By early March, the elder Guenther had sent enough for a down payment on 150 acres near the juncture of the Pedernales River and Live Oak Creek, three miles southwest of the fast-growing German community of Fredericksburg and some 60 miles northwest of San Antonio. It was, the younger Guenther thought, "the most beautiful location for a mill to be found within a radius of 20 miles." Moreover, the only mill in the entire area, that of ill-fated Mormon colonist Lyman Wight a few miles down the Pedernales, had washed away the month before.

With the encouragement of settlers now having to grind their grain by hand, he wasted no time in getting started on his own mill.

# 2. The New Mill on Live Oak Creek

The Texas Hill Country town of Fredericksburg, named for Prince Frederick of Prussia, made a congenial starting point for the ambitious young immigrant Carl Hilmar Guenther.

Fredericksburg had been established only five years before by 120 settlers as one of several towns planned by a German noblemen's' colonization company officially designated the Society for the Protection of German Immigrants in Texas. Fredericksburg founder Baron Otfried Hans Freiherr von Meusebach—he changed his name, mercifully, to John O. Meusebach—negotiated a treaty with the Comanche Indians, making the town safe for settlement. By the time Guenther arrived, its population was more than 1,000.

Fredericksburg, laid out in the manner of a Rhineland village, had a long main street lined with increasing numbers of traditional half-timbered *fachwerk* homes as temporary log dwellings were replaced. In the center was the octagonal Vereins-Kirche, a public building for the familiar German religious and social events that had so attracted Guenther to Racine, Wisconsin. Also important was dominance of the German language; "Arthur wants a letter in English," Guenther wrote home—as always, in German—of a younger brother's request, "but that cannot be accomplished at once, for I still use the dictionary."

Such frontier settlements grew up along creeks or rivers not only because of household and irrigation needs but also because water, forcefully directed, could power millstones to grind wheat for flour, freeing settlers from the sort of tedium of grinding grain by hand that was bothering Fredericksburg residents.

*(Opposite)* A sawmill had been added to Carl Hilmar Guenther's flour mill on Live Oak Creek by 1855, when his neighbor, noted Texas landscape painter Hermann Lungkwitz, did the painting from which this detail is taken. The entire painting is shown on page 98.

The octagonal Vereins-Kirche is at the center of this early photo of Fredericksburg, three miles northeast of Guenther's Live Oak Creek mill.

*Guenther's father's confidence would prove to be a crucial factor in the difficult years ahead.*

A typical frontier mill—noisy with rushing water, creaking gears and vibrating machinery, its air filled with a fine dust—could be operated by two or three men. But it had to be built and managed by a single person with the strength and abilities of a stonemason and also with the skills of an architect, carpenter, mechanic and hydraulics engineer, plus, equally as important, the savvy of a businessman.

"To make money is not given to everyone," Guenther once wrote. "It is accomplished by those who are industrious, have a good insight into things and have natural wit and are willing to take a chance."

Carl Hilmar Guenther, guild-certified master millwright from Saxony, convinced his father that even on the Comanche frontier in far-off Texas, he was up to the job. His father's confidence would prove to be a crucial factor in the difficult years ahead.

Romans two millennia before had come up with the basic milling technology Guenther would use. Europeans by the 1100s had adapted wind power as an alternative, but water power remained more dependable. Scotsman James Watt made a major modification in 1780, when he built the first steam-powered flour mill, and American Oliver Evans a few decades later figured out how to streamline the process into a single system that took in wheat at one end and produced flour at the other. But steam was not an initial option on the frontier, where millwrights operated primarily with ancient techniques.

The challenge remained to crack open the wheat kernel's tough outer shell to get at the nutritious endosperm inside. The time-honored way was to sandwich the wheat grains between two massive stones, the upper one—the *runner* stone—turning as, a fraction of an inch below it, the *bedder* stone remained stationery.

Millstones required regular dressing, a process of rechiseling grooves of the facing stones that in scissorlike fashion broke open the tough kernels of wheat and corn and made flour of the inner endosperms.

The millstones' inner surfaces were chiseled with facing patterns of grooves designed to catch the grains and, in scissorlike fashion, to break them open. Brushes at the edges of the stones swept the remains into a bin where a fine mesh (silk would do) held back the bran husks and allowed the crushed endosperms to sift through as flour into waiting sacks.

The stones required careful attention. They had to be hard enough so the facing patterns of groves did not have to be rechiseled—*dressed*—too often. The best rock for this purpose was the super-durable burr quartz quarried in the Marne Valley of northern France. Burr stones needed dressing only once or twice a year, compared to millstones of softer rock, which might require dressing every three weeks. Regardless of their makeup, the stones had to be balanced and kept precisely adjusted to prevent wear and to keep them from touching while turning, which might cause sparks that could set the mill on fire.

Typically, a mill was built beside a regularly-flowing stream at a point where a dam could form a millpond. From this reservoir, water could be diverted into a specially dug millrace. The force from the water pressure in the reservoir coupled with the decline of the millrace to create a forceful *fall* that focused pressure on the paddles of the millwheel.

If the water source was high enough, a wooden flume could extend from the end of the millrace over the top of

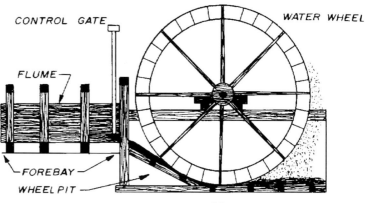

CONTROL GATE

WATER WHEEL

FLUME

FOREBAY

WHEEL PIT

UNDERSHOT WHEEL

Guenther's mill was driven by an undershot wheel, turned by water flowing through a flume leading downward to near the wheel's base.

*A bend in Live Oak Creek offered an ideal spot to accommodate the various factors involved in building a water-powered mill.*

the wheel so water hit the wheel on the far side of what was then called an *overshot* wheel. A *breastshot* wheel was hit in the center by water which then flowed out under the wheel. An *undershot* wheel was hit near the bottom.

The base of the wheels had to be high enough so gravity could carry the water past it down the millrace below the mill and back into the stream.

A mill dam had to be able to withstand flooding of the main stream. To anchor the dam during times of high water, its abutments had to remain above flood levels. The top of the dam had to be smooth enough so that, as water normally flowed over it and downstream, it would not catch debris that would act as a dam during floods. The face of the dam had to be strong enough to withstand overflowing water. And the dam had to be far enough from the mill so that if floodwaters did break the millrace's protective bypass gate or washed out the dam itself, the floodwater had room to flow around the mill and would not wash away the mill itself in the process.

Then there were the engineering calculations necessary to design the system of gears and shafts to transfer the power of the turning millwheel into the power needed to turn the millstones above and to grind the grain. The volume of water, size of the wheel and size of the stones were interrelated. An undershot millwheel 18 feet in diameter hit by water at a level three feet from its base needed to be two feet wide for every foot in diameter of the millstones.

Three miles southwest of Fredericksburg, the bend in Live Oak Creek just before it flowed into the Pedernales River—Guenther's "beautiful location for a mill"—offered a spot at the top for a dam to divert water into a millrace that would allow water to fall 16 feet onto an undershot millwheel and then rejoin the creek at the end of the bend.

At that spot, Guenther reported back to Weissenfels on March 16, 1851, "I am busy building. We cut the wood in this vicinity, which is open country, and with the help of five men have been building on the dam for eight days. Then we must dig the millrace and then the mill. I hope to be grinding in four months. . . . I could be satisfied with farming here if I did not see how well a mill would pay."

That said, he pleaded for the remainder of his inheritance: "The rest would help me so much more now than it would if I got it later when I marry, as you plan it. At that time I will not need it." Promising not to "pester" his father further once he had all of his share, he closed, noting, "My time for writing is over, as there are the men waiting to talk over the work. On weekdays I have no time and in the evening I am too tired. That is why I have to write a hasty letter when Sunday comes."

Four months later, however, the starting date was still some two months distant. "This is the hardest time!" he wrote a friend in Leipzig whom he hoped would put in a good word to his father. He would pay his father 6 percent interest to get another $500 to finish up, because, he added wryly, during the delays "the money bag contracted consumption." By the end of September Guenther had received $425 more from home, the millrace had been tested, the millstones—the finest, from France—and the waterwheel were in place and operations were only two weeks away.

Soon he could exult to the folks back home: "Now I am in a position to help myself in a dignified manner. The mill is running excellently, the machinery runs like a clock." Moreover, "Up to now I have not needed a milling engineer, for everything was built by carpenters and cabinet makers who worked by my drawings." Although Guenther had to borrow additional money to complete the mill, he could benefit from his monopoly status by upping his milling fee from one-seventh of the finished flour to one-sixth.

Guenther gave a lucid description of the operation of the wheel and gears, which he designed and had made of local wood:

"The mill is run by a waterwheel that is 16 1/2 feet high and 3 1/2 feet wide. The shaft is 2 1/2 feet thick, and the iron trunnion is 6 inches. You may well imagine that this generates a lot of power; moreover, it moves very slowly, for the stone turns 45 times while the water-wheel

Prosperous German merchant Carl Gottfried Guenther sent key financial support to his American immigrant son, Carl Hilmar Guenther, at critical points in the initial development of his son's milling company.

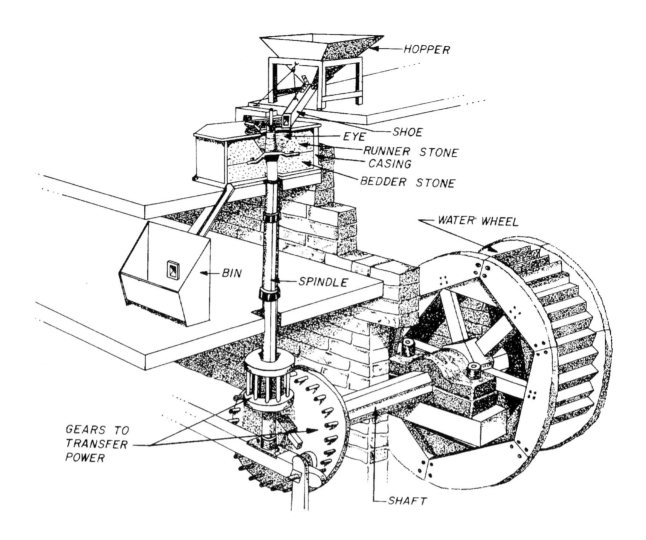

HOPPER

SHOE
EYE
RUNNER STONE
CASING
BEDDER STONE

WATER WHEEL

BIN

SPINDLE

GEARS TO
TRANSFER
POWER

SHAFT

In a typical water mill operation, wheels turned by falling water drive a mechanism of shafts and gears to turn facing millstones. The stones receive grain through the "eye" of the upper stone and grind it as flour into a bin for packaging.

revolves once. There is a cog-wheel 12 1/2 feet in diameter with 126 teeth. This is fastened onto a vertical shaft which is geared to a cog-wheel 20 inches in diameter with 16 teeth. This is fastened onto a vertical shaft at the top of which is a gearwheel 8 feet in diameter with 84 teeth. This is geared to the millstone.

"The millhouse is nice and small, 20 feet long, 16 feet wide, on the water side 27 feet high to the roof, on the entrance side 14 feet, all framed with oak beams and covered with spruce siding. The shingles are of cypress, the floor is cypress, the sills of live oak."

Before long the scene was that of prosperous rural mills elsewhere. "Often this place looks like a market place, with three to five wagons drawn by two or four yoke oxen and driven by a man on horseback," Guenther wrote. "They arrive any time between 8 and 10 o'clock. Mules and horses come and go constantly carrying bags of cornmeal and flour. Even after the customers have been attended to they often stay as long as an hour or two for a sociable visit, as this is the place where all the farmers get together. Visiting in Texas is difficult due to the long distances."

With the mill at last finished, Guenther, in his methodical fashion, could attend to more domestic matters. "It takes time and effort to accomplish anything, even to get married," he advised his father, who kept bringing it up. "It is here just like it was at home, wherever I go someone starts talking of my getting married."

He had already tried to explain, six months earlier: "Up to now I have had no time to look into that as I have had nothing on my mind but getting established in business, but from now on the problem of finding a suitable wife will gradually be taken into consideration and finally acted upon."

Parental insistence on looking for a wife with a good dowry, however, would be ignored. "In this country, I would be glad if I could find one to my taste and would gladly dispense with the dowry. . . . Here in Texas a man's wife can influence his standing and career much more easily than in Germany, because here everybody depends entirely on himself. Here it makes no difference whether a girl brings a dowry of $1,000 or of $4,000. The main thing here is what the man himself amounts to."

Guenther had, in fact, already met his future bride. The view from his log home above the mill of the gently rolling Live Oak Creek valley included ten farm homes. One was that of Hermann Lungkwitz, who became the state's first important landscape artist and did two oil paintings—in 1852 and 1855—of Guenther's mill, the first sent by Lungkwitz to Germany. Across the valley a mile to the northeast was the home of Friederich "Fritz" and Ilse Katerine Pape, German immigrants from Hanover. During his search for a mill site in 1851, Hilmar Guenther visited the well-respected Fritz Pape (the family name is still pronounced "poppy") and asked if he could stay for dinner.

"My, that man does not even wait for us to invite him to dinner," Dorothea Wilhelmine Henriette Pape, 12, the only one of the couple's four children to survive the trek from Germany, told her mother away from the others.

"Be quiet, child," her mother admonished. "That man is going to build a mill and then you will not have to grind corn every day on the hand mill."

*"It is here just like it was at home, wherever I go someone starts talking of my getting married."*

"Oh, well, if that is the case he is welcome," Dorothea replied, "but I believe that we will never get rid of him again."

Nor did they.

"Every passable girl gets married here at an early age," Guenther later explained to his parents, "so that leaves only the undesirable ones, and one of that kind is of no account as a housekeeper. . . . There are very fine German-Texan girls, but they are all too young. That would mean you would have to wait another year. In short, I will let the way of the world take its course. Spring brings roses, and time will eventually bring me the right wife."

Spring arrived four years later, when Dorothea was 16.

Early in 1855, Guenther had to reassure his parents that his fiance, Dorothea Pape, was, indeed, a nice German girl. "If I said real Texan in my letter," he wrote, "I meant that she is entirely at home here, and understands life as it is lived here. She left Germany with her parents at five years of age, so remembers nothing of that life."

Guenther went on to praise her father's prosperity and standing in the community as county treasurer ("such an office pays well"), though he confessed his fiance's fears that in education she could not measure up to his parents because her formal schooling had been cut short by the dangerous journey from Live Oak Creek.

Dorothea had been attending public school and sewing school in Fredericksburg for six months, riding "at a full gallop both coming and going," when on a return trip a mounted Indian darted from a grove of trees and grabbed at her.

"She was frightened, for she had no weapon," a granddaughter later wrote. "She was carrying her pencil box, which was a dark wooden cylinder filled with pencils. She shook this in the Indian's face, causing the pencils inside to rattle, then waved it high in the air.

"The Indian turned away and fled as fast as his horse could carry him, and she lost no time in getting home. She always thought he took the pencil box for some mysterious weapon."

That was Dorothea's last day of school in Fredericksburg. Her parents thereafter paid a tutor to come to their home, where, Guenther wrote his mother and sisters, she also "learned about neatness, diligence and economy from her mother, who is just as good a homemaker here as she had been in Germany."

*Guenther had to reassure his parents that his fiance was, indeed, a nice German girl.*

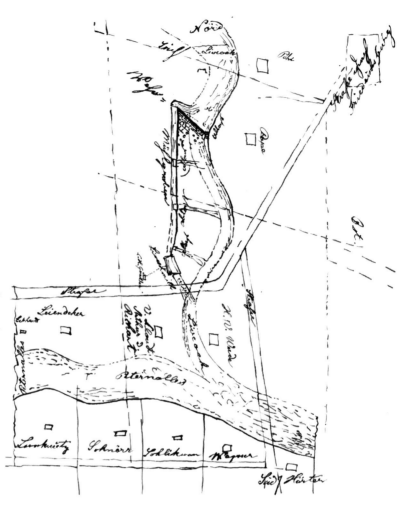

A map drawn by Carl Hilmar Guenther in an 1853 letter to his family showed how water was dammed at a bend on Live Oak Creek and sent down a mill-race, or canal, to turn the millwheel before returning to the creek above its juncture with the Pedernales River. Guenther built his home just west of the mill. To the northeast, across the creek, was the home of his future bride, Dorothea Pape. To the southwest, across the river, was the farm of Hermann Lungkwitz, the best-known early painter of Texas landscapes.

The subject of which side of the ocean they would live on never came up, for Guenther had already announced his commitment to stay in America. In 1853, the year before he received American citizenship, he wrote his mother, "I am glad that I am in Texas. I won't say that I will never see Germany again, but it never occurs to me that I would ever live there again." Guenther found it "easier here for a person to make a living and get ahead than it is in Germany" and, "best of all, it is free." In his quest he did not share the theological views of such well publicized fellow German immigrants as the Freethinkers, who opposed organized religion and dismissed the idea of a deity as irrelevant.

"Just calm yourself on that subject," Guenther wrote his concerned mother. "The first year in America I was completely stumped when it came to religion. I saw one worship what the other scorned. . . . The most honest is the copper colored Indian, who has the clearest idea of what he worships—the sun, moon and stars." Aquaintance with Freethinkers left him preferring "to keep to my religion, to which I am accustomed and in which I have been well grounded and instructed."

In 1855 Guenther replaced his small log home with a more spacious one a story and a half high, "a nice solid building" 28 feet long and 28 feet wide. Built in the style of the new plastered and whitewashed limestone rock homes dotting the countryside, it was finished and furnished in time for the couple's wedding, on October 7, 1855, in a Lutheran service.

"I consider my life since my marriage the happiest time of my entire life," Guenther soon wrote his parents, whose portraits, sent from Germany, hung in his home. Each grandfather was remembered in the naming of his and Dorothea's first child, Fritz Gottfried, born in the spring of 1857. One of his younger brothers was remembered in the naming of their second child, Arthur William, born nearly two years later.

To offset the high cost of farm labor while still keeping the family self-sufficient, Guenther used mill workers to help cultivate some ten acres near the house. He kept a dozen turkeys, two dozen chickens and several dozen hogs, plus "one very fine horse" and one or two cows—"not to mention my three dogs, which are very valuable on a place like this." Soon he was putting up a rock building as a store to sell his surplus. It could also serve to trade the animal hides he planned to export to his younger brother Gustav, who ran a tannery in Germany.

But unlike so many frontier millers who got involved in numerous other enterprises, Carl Hilmar Guenther did not allow sidelines to distract him: "With me, milling is the main thing."

Guenther was now able to concern himself more with paying off debts than with seeking cash infusions from his father. Yet he remained haunted by a disaster in 1852, scarcely a year after his mill began operations. That November, floodwaters from a violent rainstorm washed out his seven-foot-high mill dam across Live Oak Creek. There was no money in the bank with which to rebuild. The next morning, Guenther paced disconsolately up and down the creek for an hour, then made his decision.

That afternoon he began building a new dam farther upstream where it could be only two feet high and ex-

*Unlike frontier millers who got involved in many areas, Guenther stayed focused, stating, "For me, milling is the main thing."*

Their Live Oak Creek neighbor Hermann Lungkwitz made this drawing of Carl Hilmar and Dorothea Guenther in 1864, nine years after their marriage.

tended the millrace to meet it, and he had to do it all on credit. Cash in the frontier barter economy was scarce, and interest was sky-high. Those with access to money from New York or Philadelphia lent it at 20 percent interest for no more than three months at a time. Could his father lend $500 or $600 at 6 percent, payable from the day the money left Germany?

"Had I counted up my debts for you . . . you would have been afraid for me," Guenther admitted later. "Twice during that time I wanted to count up all my debts; instead, I closed the account book with a bang."

In four months—by return mail, in those days—an exceedingly grateful son received $460, at 5 percent interest. Thanks to his father's help Carl Hilmar Guenther dared open his account book again and brought it up to date. He found that during this time he had borrowed $1,000 by giving personal promissory notes, at 10 percent interest; based on his reputation for good credit, the notes themselves were being exchanged as currency by their holders. One third had since been paid off in trade with his percentage of grain ground in the reopened mill. He expected to repay more with income from the sawmill he was adding to the building. Then work on that project stopped for three months while he was ill with jaundice.

Later, in good physical health once again, the strength of the new dam proven in more high water and the sawmill in operation, Guenther could be philosophical about it all: "An occasional change gives spice to life. Anyone who has never been seriously ill has the wrong idea of life and fails to appreciate his good health. Anyone who has never been in financial difficulties fails to appreciate what he possesses."

But Carl Hilmar Guenther, a newly elected justice of the peace, was not one to pause and enjoy the status quo.

In mid-1856 Guenther was redoing his mill, adding eight feet of fall to the water by hewing a millrace "3,000 paces long" out of rock. He added a new waterwheel, 22 feet high, to power two more French millstones, hauled overland in ox-drawn wagons from the port of Indianola on the Texas Gulf coast. Even though a drought was lowering the water level, his new operation was doubling the old output. Three weeks after Guenther's reworked mill opened he owed only $600 of the $2,500 it cost, and he could look askance at three competing mills.

On one of the new competitors, a gristmill in Fredericksburg, a German immigrant from Hanover had spent his allotted $3,000 "in building and drinking," and his debt-ridden successor might end up being foreclosed upon by "our Fredericksburg Rothschild." Another, 12 miles away, was a sawmill built for $10,000 by a nephew of Dusseldorf native Hermann Altgelt, whom Guenther wrote was a New York millionaire "who wants to found a city and call it Comfort." (He did.) Guenther thought that mill was "being so badly run that it does not make expenses; one good operator could really make money there, for there is good wood in the vicinity." The third competitor, a sawmill two miles away, was "making good money."

The drought that began in 1856 was continuing, however, and no relief for mill production was foreseen until at least mid-1859, when what wheat there was would ripen. Profits that once averaged $5 a day dropped to $2 a day. Nor was there a cushion of cash reserves, all savings having been used for the expansion.

If the drought was going to reduce water below the level needed for sufficient power, Guenther knew that steam could replace it. Business picked up in 1858 to become "so-so," but Guenther could still see the advantage of putting in a steam engine if just to keep ahead of the competition. But a steam mill could handle more grain than the area was producing. So in 1859 he set out to encourage farmers to plant more wheat the next season, promising he would have a steam-powered mill ready to grind it all.

*Spreading the word about his plans for a steam mill was a miscalculation that Guenther turned to his advantage.*

When Carl Hilmar Guenther left Fredericksburg for San Antonio in 1859, he sold his mill to his father-in-law and neighbor, Fritz Pape.

Spreading the word about his plans was a miscalculation that Guenther turned to his advantage.

Fredericksburg had a group of prosperous merchants who knew that a steam mill, not requiring a major water source, could just as well be in Fredericksburg as out on Live Oak Creek. Although they had already promised Guenther that they would not build their own mill, they could also see profit for themselves in the area's increased wheat crop if they joined together and built their own mill anyway. By August 1859 the merchants had a steam mill building under construction in Fredericksburg.

Guenther wasted no time nursing hurt feelings. He quickly concluded there was not enough business around Fredericksburg for two steam mills. Moreover, several times a year he had been in San Antonio, a comparative metropolis with its 8,200 persons—more than one fourth of them German immigrants—but "only one very meager water mill."

He made his decision. "My finances are secure. My estate is well known to be the finest in County Gillespie; however, I would like to progress as fast as possible." The Live Oak Mill could be sold to his father-in-law and neighbor, Fritz Pape, to help finance a new venture, in the belief that in San Antonio "there is a real need for a good mill, which could do a marvelous business."

It was a need that Carl Hilmar Guenther, age 33, set out to fill.

Main Plaza San Antonio, Texas.

Drawn after Nature by Erhard Pentenrieder. Published by Pentenrieder & Blersch, San Antonio, Texas.

Mission San José

Mission Conception

Menger's Hotel.

Free Mason's Hall.

Alamo

Mission San Juan

German Casino.

San Antonio
July 5. 1867

Frau Rosina Guenther,
Weißenfels

Liebe Mutter!

Seit Weihnachten habe ich
keinen Brief von Euch erhalten.
Hoffentlich seid Ihr noch Alle
gesund wie beim Schreiben
Eures letzten Briefes. Meine
Frau ich u. unsere 3 Knaben
u. 3 Mädchen sind alle wohl.
Wir haben gestern sehr vergnügten
4ten July gefeiert u. sind heute
Morgen bei Tage verbracht nach Hause
gekommen. Seit dem Kriege hat es
sich in San Antonio sehr verändert.
Jeder Ball verlangt mein Damenkoi,
letten die weisten Nummern des
Bazar werden von den Damen gestickt

# 3. Opportunity in San Antonio

Carl Hilmar Guenther was not the only entrepreneur to sense opportunity in frontier San Antonio in the 1850s. The capital of the Spanish province of Texas only eight decades before, San Antonio had a new lease on life thanks to Texas joining the United States and the arrival of the U.S. Army in the city. The promise of stability unleashed a rush of new settlers.

San Antonio, still the principal town in Texas, was founded in 1718 as a waystation between Spanish mission strongholds along the Rio Grande and new missions on the French Louisiana frontier. The verdant spot near the headwaters of the San Antonio River drew no fewer than five Spanish missions, though their priests' messages of peace and harmony were insufficient to keep revolutionaries and established regimes from quarreling over the strategic town.

First, Mexican insurgents sought to take San Antonio from the Spanish crown. Then Texas revolutionaries sought to overthrow the incumbent Mexican government, a fray that brought the president of Mexico, Antonio de López de Santa Anna, to San Antonio in 1836 as head of the army that annihilated the band of Texans fortified in the old Alamo mission.

Even though Texas managed to win independence, it was not until 1848, after the Mexican War ended and Texas was firmly annexed to the United States, that San Antonio was freed from the threat of raids from below the Rio Grande. By then only 800 San Antonians were left, leaving the place to be described in 1849 by a visiting future president of the United States, Rutherford B. Hayes, as "an old, ruined Spanish town."

*(Opposite)* San Antonio's appealing "odd and antiquated foreignness" proved a fertile field for engravers of this letterhead, used by Carl Hilmar Guenther for a letter home in 1867 after his family celebrated the Fourth of July and arrived home at dawn. Here he writes, in German: "San Antonio has changed since the war. Every ball demands new gowns for the ladies. Imagine! They study the Bazaar faithfully and then try out every new style."

San Antonio's river managed to power a few mills as it meandered through town, as shown in this bird's-eye view looking southeast in 1873. Guenther's home and his first local mill is at the top right corner of the view, between the sharp bend at the end of King William Street. Closer in, on the far side at Arsenal Street, can be spotted his Upper Mill, built in 1868.

Only ten years later, when Carl Hilmar Guenther arrived to buy land for a flour mill, waves of diverse newcomers had transformed San Antonio into a bustling outpost of more than 8,000 people, "the busiest city in Texas," he wrote. In its geographic isolation—a railroad from the coast was still a quarter-century away—San Antonio maintained a distinctive ambience termed by one enthralled visitor, Frederick Law Olmsted, who would

soon design New York City's Central Park, as "an odd and antiquated foreignness."

Although the new San Antonians represented a broad range of ethnic and geographic origins, a large proportion were born in Germany, where the political situation continued to offend natives seeking greater personal and political freedom. In the time since Guenther's departure from Germany, one such immigrant, Johann Nicholaus Simon Menger, had established San Antonio's first indus-

DAUGHTERS OF THE REPUBLIC OF TEXAS LIBRARY AT THE ALAMO

One colorful spot in remote mid-nine-teenth-century San Antonio was Military Plaza, where an open-air vegetable market and food stands mingled with hay wagons and stagecoaches bound for the distant frontier.

try, a soap factory. A cousin, William Menger, opened the state's first commercial brewery in San Antonio and also the city's leading hotel. Dr. Julius Heusinger opened the city's first drugstore.

The vibrant German community, which already enjoyed the state's first formally organized male singing society, formed—with 106 German immigrant members—the Casino Club, San Antonio's first social club and theater. Children were assured a good education at the German-English School, established by Casino Club members in 1858. The German community's activity was chronicled in a German language newspaper, the *San Antonio Zeitung*.

So Guenther could feel right at home on August 26, 1859, when he closed the deal on a mill site on a small peninsula formed by a sharp bend of the river less than a mile south of the center of town.

Though the San Antonio River's flow was never strong enough to support the sort of large mills that lined broader rivers in cities elsewhere in the nation, during most of the nineteenth century the flow powered small mills, which were sufficient for the local populace. In pre–Civil War Texas there were no other large populations to

THE UNIVERSITY OF TEXAS INSTITUTE OF TEXAN CULTURES ATSAN ANTONIO,
COURTESY THOMAS W. CUTRER

The San Antonio region's first flour mill was built in the 1790s at Mission San José, as shown in this 1930s drawing by Carl Hilmar Guenther's grandson Ernst Schuchard, who used his milling knowledge to aid in its restoration. Water flowed to the mill from the mission's *acequia*, a narrow ditch, shown above, typical of those engineered by Spaniards to divert water from the San Antonio River.

serve, and no good transportation system to get to them had there been any. Nor around San Antonio was there an overwhelming supply of wheat to be ground, since there were fewer crop-rich farms than surrounded Fredericksburg. San Antonio's more arid outlands favored range use for cattle, sheep and goats.

Milling in San Antonio had been a minor enterprise since Franciscan friars built the region's first flour mill at Mission San José in the 1790s, reflecting the European in-spired reorientation of mission Indians' diets from corn to wheat. The small mill managed to operate on a tiny reser-voir of water from one of the Spanish *acequias*, carefully engineered lateral ditches extending from the river into adjoining neighborhoods and fields. So did a second mill, built by the Yturri family in the 1820s on land formerly belonging to Mission Concepción.

North of town, two burr stones given to local colonists by the King of Spain ground grain until the early nine-teenth century in a whitewashed building known as the Molino Blanco. In 1849 the abandoned stones were sal-vaged for a mill near the center of town by Nathaniel Lewis, a real estate promoter, merchant and politician who also found time to be a cattleman. Milling for Lewis was a sideline, and the lack of a strong focus caused his mill to be termed a "very meager" operation by Carl Hilmar Guenther, for whom milling remained "the main thing."

In addition to his concentration on milling, Guenther's success at getting established in San Antonio was aided by

DRT LIBRARY AT THE ALAMO

In 1859 the Guenthers moved into their new home overlooking the San Antonio River and the site of their new mill. The rear of the house, below, later became the front, as a new neighborhood moved toward the home and a new addition covered the original front facade.

three other factors, not all of them wished for. His benevolent father, in declining health for several years, died in Germany in the spring of 1859. The younger Guenther could now count on more inheritance to help finance a new venture. Operations of the Live Oak Creek mill, though diminished by drought-induced crop shortages, could still support the family. And transfers of funds from overseas could be completed, equipment ordered from the East and a mill built within the narrow window of time before the looming Civil War cut supply lines and disrupted communications.

After paying $500 down and borrowing another $2,000 to tide him over until his inheritance arrived, Guenther focused on the first order of business—a home for the family of four. The two-story, six-room home was built of limestone blocks quarried north of San Antonio on the future site of the zoo in Brackenridge Park. Lower rooms were partly below ground level, insulated from the summer heat. Like the old home on Live Oak Creek, it faced the stream and the mill, as there were no other homes nearby.

The move from Fredericksburg, a 60-mile trek that could take as many as five days by wagon, was not without trauma. After the family settled in, Guenther wrote that his wife, Dorothea, then 19, "suffers so much more homesickness than I could ever have imagined possible," though ever-cosmopolitan San Antonio was stimulating to the children. Their older son, Fritz, two and a half, "speaks very distinctly, but occasionally mixes Spanish, German and English all together."

As the family watched from their new home, work progressed on the mill. The mill on Live Oak Creek cut

Jacobson, pho.    400. BEAUTIES OF SAN ANTONIO RIVER.    2.E. HOUSTON ST. SAN ANTONIO.

The dam for Guenther's main Lower Mill—down a millrace and out of sight—remained a scenic spot even though it was soon eclipsed in picturesqueness upstream by his second mill, which stood beside its millpond.

the timbers and ground flour for the young household, and their old farm kept the Guenthers supplied with meat and butter. Cash remained hard to come by. There was not enough to pay carpenters and builders, but a dam had to be built and a 150-yard millrace needed to be dug through soft limestone 20 feet deep across the small peninsula formed by the river.

Struggling farmers in the new colony of Alsatian immigrants around Castroville 20 miles west proved to be the solution. As wheat growers, they were a major potential source of business. Guenther persuaded a number of them to come with their mules, picks, shovels and camping gear to his new mill site, where their labor was rewarded with credit on the books of his future operation.

By mid-April 1860, two months ahead of the local wheat harvest, the new mill was in partial operation, slowed only by the delay of a machinery shipment from New York. By the end of the year the financial picture improved with arrival of part of Guenther's inheritance from Germany ($1,500), sale of the livestock and grain supply at the Live Oak Creek farm ($2,300) and sale of the Live Oak Creek mill to Guenther's father-in-law, Fritz Pape, for

The deep millrace dug by Alsatians from Castroville carried water from the river to power Guenther's first San Antonio mill, at top, which opened in 1860.

$4,000 ($1,000 down); Guenther was certain he could have sold the mill before the drought for more than $10,000.

Knowing that he could grind more wheat than was available locally, Guenther began importing ox-drawn wagonloads of wheat—some from Mexico—and expanding retail sales of sacked flour to the San Antonio market. Thus began a pivotal shift for the company, a redirection from simply serving the grinding needs of farmers to filling the flour and baking needs of consumers.

But before he could fully capitalize on this strategy, Guenther's mill had to survive the Civil War.

San Antonio remained far from combat, though its residents were divided. Anglo-American immigrants from the South were able to pass the Texas secession ordinance in San Antonio, but by only a narrow margin. The proposition met with strong opposition particularly from German immigrants, who opposed slavery but still wanted to get along with their neighbors. To avoid public identification with the antislavery issue, so many German immi-

TOP: WITTE MUSEUM, SAN ANTONIO, TEXAS;
BELOW: UT INSTITUTE OF TEXAN CULTURES

In the mid-1870s Carl Hilmar and Dorothea Guenther posed for a Commerce Street photographer with their seven children. Standing, from left, are Marie Dorothea, Fritz, Hilmar Louis, Amanda, Arthur and Erhard (front). Mathilda is seated in the center.

*Short of silk during the Civil War, Guenther purchased a wedding dress from a jilted bride and used it to sift flour.*

grant businessmen canceled their advertising in the abolitionist *San Antonio Zeitung* that in 1861 the beleagured newspaper closed.

Guenther wrote his mother that "a fierce political battle" on the subject was also raging in Fredericksburg. Apparently worried that her letters to him might be inspected, he asked, "When you write, please do not mention anything about our political problems."

As a miller, Guenther was exempted from military service, though required to furnish flour to the Confederate Army and its troops in San Antonio. Shortages had to be contended with. When the mill ran out of the cloth needed to sift the flour from the chaff, Guenther purchased a billowing wedding dress from a jilted bride and used its silk as sifting cloth. To shield his profits from the instabilities of Confederate currency, he fell back on his German connections and paid traveling friends to carry his funds from San Antonio to a Leipzig bank. During the war the family's number of children grew to five with the births of a third son, Hilmar Louis, and two daughters, Amanda Auguste and Marie Dorothea.

War's end found San Antonio again on the brink of rapid growth, with Guenther poised to join in. His mill was established, his capital was secure. By 1868 his family was complete with the birth of a third daughter, Mathilda Hulda, and a fourth son, Erhard Rosini, his middle name the masculine form of Guenther's mother's name, Rosina. In 1867 Guenther made the most of hot South Texas summers by branching into the field of ice manufacture, with two ice machines taking advantage of water from the river.

Beside the San Antonio River on Guenther's mill grounds, where this picture was apparently taken in 1874, was a favorite spot for picnics and songfests. Carl Hilmar Guenther is seated at the guitar player's right.

*(Opposite)* Needing to increase production but lacking sufficient water power at his original location, in 1868 Guenther built a second mill a quarter-mile upstream, its wide waterwheel visible in the above view. This Upper Mill, closer to town, became both mills' primary retail sales and distribution point (below) for flour and cornmeal.

By 1868 Guenther needed to increase production, but the flow of water at his mill was insufficient to power more stones. So he built a second mill a quarter mile upstream, across from the United States Arsenal. Conveniently, a natural barrier of rocks at a waterfall needed only a little mortar to fill the gaps and create a dam, raising the water level six inches for a millpond.

The newly designated Upper Mill's stones, specially grooved for milling corn and rye flour, were soon expanded to three pairs. The picturesque one and a half-story frame mill and its wheel beside the millpond became a favorite subject for painters and photographers.

The Lower Mill, which ground only wheat, was expanded. Retail sales for both mills—known collectively as Guenther's Mills—were set up in a new frame building by the Upper Mill as the town grew toward it.

Soon Guenther found himself at the edge of the most fashionable German neighborhood in San Antonio, as elaborate homes of prospering immigrants were built down a bend of the river. The main residential street was named King Wilhelm—after Prussia's Wilhelm I—by new resident Ernst Hermann Altgelt, the "millionaire" who had laid out the Hill Country town of Comfort and whose nephew was an early competitor of Guenther's near Fredericksburg. Non-Germans referred to the neighborhood as the Little Rhine, or more irreverently, as Sauerkraut Bend.

Only a few rocks remain to hold back a semblance of the downtown millpond that once provided water to Guenther's original San Antonio competitor, Nat Lewis's mill. Its wooden wheel was stilled when the mill's dam was removed in a flood-control measure in 1869.

A border of wheat encircles the design on a sack of the finest flour made by Guenther's Mills, named Guenther's Best in 1875.

The grounds of Guenther's Mills became favorite picnic spots, although the grounds of which mill were not specified in reports of two events. On one Sunday afternoon in 1876, San Antonio residents of Swiss origin held a picnic, complete with choral singing and fireworks after dark, to benefit victims of a flood in Switzerland.

The year before, a group of San Antonio visitors sufficiently important to be accompanied by a newspaper reporter dropped by "to examine the water power, so they said," wrote the reporter. "Mr. Guenther seemed to take in the situation at a glance. With true German hospitality he rushed into the cellar and soon appeared weighed down with Rhine wine and Anheuser's St. Louis beer, which he placed on the grass." Whether or not this was an early exercise in media relations, the event gained favorable mention in the next edition.

Carl Hilmar Guenther was not alone in seeking to capitalize on San Antonio's growing market for flour. A formidable competitor was the new five-story stone Laux Mill with its massive iron undershot wheel, built in 1860 beside the river near the center of town on the future site of the Milam Building. In 1871 the Alamo Mill, powered by a 60-inch turbine waterwheel, opened along the river on the northern edge of town near the onetime location of the Molino Blanco.

Nature intervened to cause the closing of Guenther's original competitor, the Lewis mill at the Navarro Street river crossing. That mill's pond was formed by a Spanish-

WITTE MUSEUM, SAN ANTONIO, TEXAS

*One competing mill shut down after its dam was removed in a flood-control effort.*

era dam, built to raise the river level so water could enter the acequia flowing south to irrigate the fields around Mission Concepción two miles away.

The Lewis mill's dam, however, also slowed rising water and exacerbated flooding in the center of town, as became apparent during a deluge in 1865. Guenther's dams to the south were not yet thought to be a problem, but engineers fingered the Lewis/Concepción dam as a major hazard. In 1869 the city ordered it removed, causing the mill, without a reservoir for water power, to shut down.

Such local competitive factors would soon, however, be of minor concern, as San Antonio was finally linked to the rest of the nation by rail and a new era abruptly began.

# 4. Coping with Change

Life in San Antonio would change dramatically in the last quarter of the nineteenth century, as a new railroad connected the city with the rest of the nation. No longer would cumbersome ox-drawn wagon, horseback and stagecoach be the sole means of access.

More than half of the 15,000 San Antonians were on hand when the first train pulled in from Houston on February 19, 1877. The celebration lasted two days.

If Carl Hilmar Guenther were among the celebrants, he would have been wise enough to temper his enthusiasm with a cold realization of the implications of the event. For the future of Guenther's Mills would depend upon how he dealt with upcoming challenges of new competition from the outside world, as well as with the rapid changes in milling technology.

The railroad might make it easier for Guenther to import wheat and export flour, but it also gave other Texas mills as well as the great mills of the midwestern grain belt access to the South Texas market. These mills were continually upgrading their equipment as a flurry of new inventions began streamlining the long-static flour milling process.

Recognizing that he could lose his competitive edge, Guenther began replacing his original Lower Mill building with one twice its size.

By the end of 1877 a Milwaukee milling machinery manufacturer was installing the new equipment, powered not by an old-style open waterwheel but by a turbine wheel five feet high and six feet in diameter enclosed in a casing able to capture the once-lost power of water splashed away. Now power would go to the millstones not via

*(Opposite)* In response to the rapid growth following arrival of the railroad in San Antonio in 1877, Carl Hilmar Guenther replaced his 1859 mill with this larger, three-story building on the same site. Replacement of the old waterwheel with water-powered turbines also increased productivity.

With increased prosperity in the 1880s, the Upper Mill building (center) was joined by others.

Although wheat production was increasing with replacement of hand scythes by mechanical horse-drawn reapers, repeated droughts in South Texas led to the import of wheat from other regions.

an antiquated system of wooden gears but through a system of flexible belts. Four pairs of millstones were install-ed, raising the mill's daily capacity to 77 barrels. When the mill opened in the spring of 1878, one newspaper reported that its output was "equal to the entire consumption of San Antonio."

Soon the Upper Mill's picturesque waterwheel was also replaced, with a turbine once used in the waterworks in latter-day Brackenridge Park.

Weather interfered with the benefits of the new efficiency as a drought drastically lowered local wheat production in 1878–79. Bringing in grain from elsewhere offset the sort of drought-induced production drop Guenther had suffered on Live Oak Creek 20 years earlier, though the added rail costs cut down profits. This happened again during a drought in 1881–83.

In the 1880s San Antonio's population soared past 30,000, fully one–fourth of them German immigrants and their children. The Guenthers' neighborhood was the residential heart of a close-knit German-speaking community having a social life all of its own, with singing societies, hunting clubs and fraternal organizations. As the seven Guenther children married, all of the spouses turned out to be first- or second-generation Germans except for Hilmar Louis's wife, Marie, who was born in Switzerland. All seven families ended up in homes within a few blocks of the main Guenther home.

Nor were ties with the old country forgotten; during the mid-1870s, older sons Fritz and Arthur had completed their education while living with their paternal grandmother in Weissenfels, Germany.

The process of keeping the milling business in the family began in July 1878, when Guenther's Mills became C. H. Guenther & Sons, as Fritz, 21, and Arthur, 19, joined

DRT LIBRARY AT THE ALAMO

Three of the four homes in this 1880s picture were among those in the King William neighborhood occupied by the growing Guenther family. The view is west along Guenther Street from the corner of Madison Street. At far left is the home of Adolph and Amanda Guenther Wagner, at far right that of Albert and Marie Guenther Beckmann. Second from left is the first Guenther home. The three still stand; the fourth was razed in 1967 for plant expansion.

their father in a formal partnership. Fritz managed the business end while Arthur focused on operations. The senior Guenther held ownership of the properties and inventory while each son got a salary and paid rent to the partnership. Half the profits went to the father and the rest were split by the sons. A year later the sons got 8 percent interest for leaving their shares of the profits—$1,000 each—in the business.

As his father had respected the judgement and independence of a thoughtful if restless son, so did Carl Hilmar Guenther now keep a light rein on his own sons.

I make a point of pushing my children ahead even if occasionally they make mistakes," he wrote. "Those mistakes do not matter. Through them they learn to watch more closely. . . . In this manner the boys will gain their independence and at the same time relieve me of a lot of work."

Guenther's pace was being slowed by a severe case of asthma, from which his father had suffered and as already did his pre-teenage son, Erhard. "Every day I have to spend hours lying on the sofa, waiting for it to subside and the cough to wear off," Guenther wrote in 1874. "After such a siege I feel well again."

C. H. Guenther & Sons prospered during the 1880s as the San Antonio and Aransas Pass Railroad built a trestle across the river to the doors of the Lower Mill. The number of millhands grew to 20, the nonrail distribution system to six teams of horses. By 1887 the Lower Mill's daily production capacity was up to 120 barrels of flour, while the Upper Mill's reached 400 bushels of rye flour and cornmeal.

Water discharged through the turbines helped make a fine swimming hole beside Guenther's Lower Mill.

Emphasis on quality remained high. At the San Antonio International Exposition in 1888, C. H. Guenther & Sons won first premiums for the best bushel of wheat bran, best bushel of Mediterranean wheat, best bushel of wheat–other varieties and best bushel of red rust-proof oats, plus a second premium for best bushel of rye and a silver medal for best barrel of straight flour.

By 1891 Guenther at last felt comfortable enough with everything to take his wife, Dorothea, and their youngest child, Erhard, on a summer trip to Europe, though his beloved mother had died eight years before. It was his first time back since he slipped away 43 years before.

"We have now visited all the relatives," Dorothea wrote her father from Dresden at the end of June. "Up to now we have had a most wonderful time. Erhard attends to all the details and our plans have clicked like clockwork. . . . [Hilmar] showed us a mill where he had worked in his youth, and also the store where he bought his first spectacles. . . . The annual fair is on here for eight days, and there is so much life in town. . . . I think of you and our good Mother who told us so often about these fairs. But who would ever have dreamed that I would see it with my own eyes?"

But back in San Antonio a decade awaited that would see the family's milling operation, though revolutionized, threatened by defection and unexpected loss.

PIONEER FLOUR MILLS 100th ANNIVERSARY ALBUM, ERNST SCHUCHARD PAPERS, DRT LIBRARY

A railroad trestle spanning the river and a shorter one across the millrace, above, brought the ease of rail shipments to the door of the Lower Mill in the 1880s. The mill's flour was also winning medals.

The year after his return from Europe, Guenther oversaw replacement of some of the Lower Mill's old millstones with six stands of steel rollers, a system first implemented in Minneapolis in 1878. The new process first crushed the grain between corrugated steel cylinders. Then, using a more gradual reduction, after initial sifting the remaining flour was crushed between smooth steel cylinders to produce finer grades.

Rollers eliminated altogether the cost in downtime and the labor of dressing the old millstones. They also ground flour more quickly, allowed greater control and increased production by some 5 percent.

No San Antonio competitor could keep up. By 1890 the Laux Mill, the Alamo Mill and even the old Lewis Mill, revived in 1880 under new ownership with a steam engine, had all closed. The possibility of a competitor emerging from within the family must have been farthest from Guenther's mind.

Second son Arthur William Guenther, 38, however, soon decided to use his mechanical expertise to better advantage by opening his own mill with Gustav Giesecke, 29, a brother-in-law of his wife. His father, after all, was no stranger to the drive for independence and should understand his son's feelings.

In mid-1894, Arthur Guenther sold his share of the family mill and property to his older brother, Fritz. Two miles north, along the International & Great Northern Railroad, Arthur and his brother-in-law put up a building they named Liberty Mills, operated by a steam engine with a daily capacity of 100 barrels. C. H. Guenther & Sons immediately became C. H. Guenther & Son.

Three men whose presidencies of the Guenther family's mills spanned 103 years—Carl Hilmar Guenther, Erhard Guenther and Adolph Beckmann—are among those gathered beside the Guenther House in 1893.

Pictured are, from left, top: Albert F. Beckmann holding his son Albert, Arthur W. Guenther, Mathilde Guenther (Mrs. Hermann) Schuchard, Hermann Schuchard, Fritz Guenther, Helena Peltzer (Mrs. Fritz) Guenther, Erhard Guenther, Marie Bachmann (Mrs. Hilmar Louis) Guenther and Hilmar Louis Guenther;

center row, Marie Guenther (Mrs. Albert F.) Beckmann, Elise Groos (Mrs. Arthur W.) Guenther, Dorothea Pape (Mrs. C. H.) Guenther, Fritz Pape, Carl Hilmar Guenther, Amanda Guenther (Mrs. Adolph) Wagner and Adolph Wagner;

front, Adolph Beckmann, Regina Beckmann (Mrs. Laurence Hurst), Helena Guenther (Mrs. Arthur Muir), Ernst Otto Guenther and Hilmar Gustav Guenther.

In the family parlor at right, Carl von Iwonski's portraits of the elder Guenthers hang above his piano. A portrait of her father, Fritz Pape, hangs to the right of the door.

Two years later, in mid-1896, the competitors called a truce and formed a two-year trial operating partnership called The C. H. Guenther Milling Company. The new entity rented the mills from the existing companies and shared expenses and profits. Carl Hilmar Guenther was president, without specific duties, although, the agreement stated, "his decision will be final in all important matters." Fritz Guenther was vice president, Arthur Guenther was superintendent in charge of production and Gustav

This peaceful detail from a Liberty Bell Flour advertisement belies the tension of the time between Carl Hilmar Guenther and his second son, Arthur; in 1898 C. H. Guenther & Son sued The Guenther Milling Company, and the breakaway son's company sued back.

Giesecke was secretary in charge of the office and workers, sharing responsibility for product pricing with Vice President Fritz Guenther.

But in December 1897, Fritz Guenther, 40, died after an illness of eight months, leaving a wife and daughters, ages three and eight; a third child, a son, had died in July at the age of 15 months. An added sorrow was the death from cancer in mid-1898 of Dorothea Pape Guenther, Carl Hilmar's wife of 43 years. She was 58.

Fritz's widow, Helena, took her husband's place as vice president of The C. H. Guenther Milling Company to represent herself and her young children. However, when the trial partnership expired nine months later, in September 1898, all parties agreed not to renew it. Then things headed downhill.

The big problem involved the use of brand names. During the partnership, C. H. Guenther & Son and Liberty Mills shared production of the same brands. When the partnership ended, C. H. Guenther & Son went back to producing only its previous brands.

Arthur Guenther and Gustav Giesecke formed a new corporation with Conrad A. Goeth, husband of their wives' first cousin and an attorney. Rather than reverting to Liberty Mills, they dropped the "C. H." in the newly ended partnership's name and became The Guenther Milling Company. They continued using, however, not just their old Liberty Mills brand names but also the C. H. Guenther & Son brand names, which apparently were not registered as trademarks. Especially irksome to Carl Hilmar Guenther was his competitor's use of Guenther's Best, which he had assigned to his own top grade back in 1875.

C. H. Guenther & Son sued The Guenther Milling Company in November 1898. The breakaway son's company sued back.

Nine months later, the two companies reached a settlement in district court: none of the seven contested brand names would be used by either company without the unanimous agreement of all parties. Old names like Guenther's Best, Guenther's Patent and Guenther's Bakers were effectively consigned to the dustbin.

But by then the issue was moot. In March 1899 C. H. Guenther & Son had joined the national parade of mills giving zippier names to flour brands than Best, Patent or Bakers. In Minneapolis, the Washburn-Crosby Company had named its top brand Gold Medal. In Knoxville, Ten-

Following the defection of Arthur and the death of Fritz, listed on the statement at top, came the shift reflected below from C. H. Guenther & Sons to C. H. Guenther & Son, Inc. Erhard and his brother-in-law Adolph Wagner aided founder C. H. Guenther, whose likeness was promoted to distinguish the original company from the competition.

nessee, J. Allen Smith and Company had named its best-selling grade White Lily. C. H. Guenther & Son went right to a prime attribute—longevity—for the new name of its most popular brand: Pioneer.

To make sure there was no mistaking that Pioneer was made by the original Guenther company, onto every barrelhead and sack went a likeness of its bearded founder, C. H. Guenther. And just in case anyone in northern Mexico might miss the point, underneath the portrait went a caption: "El Viejo," Spanish for "The Old Man."

Other newly minted C. H. Guenther brands were Dewey's Success, with uniformed Spanish-American War hero Admiral George Dewey pictured on the sacks; Hoo-Hoo, named for a popular serenade; Alamo Brand, bearing a picture of the Alamo; Golden Harvest, featuring a sheaf of wheat; White Wings, with a drawing of a white wing dove clutching blades of wheat in its feet; Texana, showing a Texas flag; and Angel Food, with an angel portrayed amid roses. Our Big was a baking flour.

The finest—and most expensive—grades were "patent" flours, whiter products made by setting the rollers farther apart and regrinding middlings after they passed through a purifier that removed remaining bran. Pioneer named its patent flours Magnolia, Never Fail and World Breaker.

All brand names were formally adopted as trademarks by C. H. Guenther & Son, incorporated at the end of 1898 with a new family hierarchy. Fritz had died and the trial partnership with Arthur's company had failed. But there were two more brothers. Hilmar Louis Guenther, 36, was a banker in Austin and had no interest in milling. He was, though, willing to return home and take over as his share of the family business the nearby Southern Ice and Cold

Reorganizing in the face of new competition, Carl Hilmar Guenther's milling company positioned itself as the pioneer, so naming its lead brand and adding the founder's picture on barrel-head labels and sacks for added impact. Among the 11 other brands also trade-marked in 1899 was Magnolia, a high-grade patent flour.

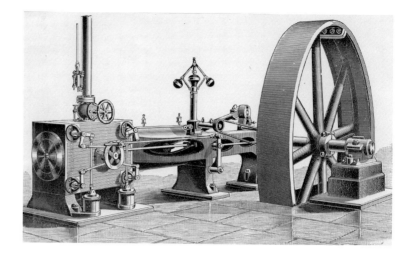

Urged forward by the threat of competition, Carl Hilmar Guenther, schooled in ancient milling techniques, kept up with modern technology. In 1892 he supplemented hand-hewn millstones with steel rollers that crushed grain with a new precision and required far less maintenance. Two years later he augmented water power from the increasingly undependable San Antonio River's flow with energy from the latest Bates-Corliss steam engine.

Storage Company, the prospering outgrowth of his father's venture into ice manufacturing three decades earlier.

Erhard Rosini Guenther, 29, a Washington and Lee College graduate who had married Josephine Charlotte "Lottie" Harnisch and was practicing law in San Antonio, agreed to take over the mills.

Carl Hilmar Guenther formally became president of C. H. Guenther & Son Inc., and Erhard was named vice president and general manager. Adolph Wagner, husband of eldest daughter Amanda, was named secretary. The elder Guenther kept no stock for himself but saw majority ownership go to those involved in daily operations—three-eighths to Erhard and two-eighths to the Wagners. His other daughters—Marie (Mrs. Albert) Beckmann and Mathilda (Mrs. Hermann) Schuchard—and Fritz's widow, Helena Peltzer Guenther, each received one-eighth.

Up the tracks at The Guenther Milling Company, Arthur Guenther remained president as his wife's family's role expanded. His brother in law Gustav Giesecke stayed secretary while another brother in law, Werner Wilkins, became treasurer. Keeping an eye on the three was a new chairman—none other than their father in law, noted San Antonio banker and 1848 German immigrant Frederick Groos, 71.

But the upstart company was doomed for the rest of its existence to play catch-up. It was no easy road even at the outset, as Carl Hilmar Guenther showed his old fire. When the new competitor opened with a steam engine, the patriarch got one, too, a sleek coal-burning Bates-Corliss model that assured a steady source of energy; increased drilling of artesian wells for water-hungry San

    BOTH: PIONEER FLOUR MILLS 100th ANNIVERSARY ALBUM, ERNST SCHUCHARD PAPERS, DRT LIBRARY

*By the time of his death in 1902 at the age of 76, Carl Hilmar Guenther had some assurance that his heirs could manage successfully in the century ahead.*

Antonio was shrinking the San Antonio River and making its water power undependable.

Then Guenther installed new sifting equipment, said to be the second of its type manufactured in the United States, and the Lower Mill's daily capacity grew to 600 barrels.

Guenther's latest plan for succession was working. As Erhard Guenther assumed operational control, he began consolidating Upper and Lower Mill operations at the Lower Mill, which in 1900 gained an additional building, a three-story brick mill with a 200-horsepower engine—among the largest in the city—and a daily capacity of 300 barrels. This replaced production of the picturesque but outmoded Upper Mill, closed and rented in 1901—at $40 per month plus $10 monthly for turbine power—to become Edward Dreiss's San Antonio Pasta Works, a manufacturer of macaroni.

As a young man, Carl Hilmar Guenther had left an old country burdened with old ways. He crossed the ocean to sample life in various regions of a new land, finding in Texas the place most likely to give the highest return on his talents and ambitions. He worked hard, capitalizing on advantages and opportunities but not neglecting qualities of life for his growing family.

By the time of his death on October 2, 1902, at the age of 76, Carl Hilmar Guenther had some assurance that his heirs were capable of navigating the growing company through the uncharted shoals of the coming century.

# 5. A New Generation

Erhard Guenther, the "Son" in C. H. Guenther & Son, posed with a sheaf of wheat while on a trip through West Texas with a great-niece in 1941.

(*Opposite*) Pioneer Flour Mills kept a high profile during Fiesta parades in the early 20th century. A photographer snapped this float at the mill as it was about to be drawn in the 1906 parade.

At the dawn of the twentieth century, rapidly changing technology and ever-tougher competition were causing a sharp decline in the number of family-owned mills. The newly restructured C. H. Guenther & Son, Incorporated, however, not only survived but continued to grow under its second president and general manager, Erhard Rosini Guenther.

The good-natured Erhard Guenther, youngest son of Carl Hilmar and Dorothea Pape Guenther, stood two inches above six feet, was large-boned and almost portly. Despite his size, he was light on his feet and loved to dance; he brought the noted dance instructor Bud Nash to San Antonio and paid for lessons for his great-nieces and great-nephews.

Erhard Guenther's paternalistic benevolence extended beyond his family to the mill workers, helping him early on to establish a strong team of lifetime employees, liberally laced with relatives. A first cousin on his mother's side, Arthur Storms, was his longtime sales manager. On his father's side, two brothers-in-law served at the officer level, Adolph Wagner as vice president and secretary—through 1934—and Hermann Schuchard, treasurer until 1945.

Erhard Guenther and his family moved into the home his parents built adjacent to the mill, at the foot of King William Street on what was named Guenther Street. There he and his wife maintained the tradition of family Christmas Eve gatherings in the Guenther home beside the mill. The Wagners and Schuchards lived in homes on adjoining lots, other cousins down nearby streets.

A third generation was also coming into the business. Carl Hilmar Guenther's grandson Adolph G. Beckmann joined the mill as a machinery oiler in 1907, at the age of 19. He would eventually serve as president, as would an-

OPPOSITE: ERNST SCHUCHARD PAPERS 6/5, DRT LIBRARY; ABOVE: HELENA HURST HARRISON

Packers pose with their sacks inside C. H. Guenther & Son's new three-story brick mill in 1908.

other grandson, Ernst Schuchard, longtime head milling engineer. That so many relatives could live and work so closely to each other in harmony as managers, directors and owners over such a long period of time strengthened the company chances for survival. At the beginning of the century there were some 250 independent flour mills in Texas. At mid-century there were fewer than 60.

Helping fuel the expansion of C. H. Guenther & Son in these years was the rapid growth of San Antonio, largest

city in Texas. When the century's first decade ended in 1910, San Antonio's population had grown by an amazing 81 percent, from 53,000 to 97,000. Ten years later the rate had slowed to 67 percent, but the city's population passed 160,000. The demand for flour, cornmeal and livestock feed far outstripped the region's supply of grain, by now routinely brought in by rail from northern Texas, Oklahoma and Kansas.

To the south, the Rio Grande Valley was also booming, as hordes of newly arrived fruit growers seized upon new irrigation methods to develop what was being promoted as the state's Winter Garden. By developing a mobile sales force and an efficient delivery system, C. H. Guenther & Son maintained a strong presence throughout Texas and northern Mexico.

During all this, the main competition became the giant milling companies of the midwestern grain belt, in particular Pillsbury and General Mills. "Why do San Antonians buy Kansas City flour and other grain products when the San Antonio mills put up the very finest grades of flour it is possible to purchase?" asked the San Antonio Manufacturers' Club in an appeal, not to the "man of the house" but to the housewife, "the power behind the household."

In listing other local products at least the equal of those produced elsewhere, the group concluded, "It does not seem possible that this negligence could be intentional on the part of the housekeeper; it is probably mere thoughtlessness."

Once such lapses were overcome, C. H. Guenther & Son still had to distinguish itself from its only local competition, the annoyingly named Guenther Milling Company. Over there, C. H. Guenther & Son President Erhard Guenther's brother Arthur left Guenther Milling in 1912 to become a vice president at his wife's family's Groos National Bank. The Guenther name, however, was becoming less visible at both companies, as each sought identification with its best-selling brand.

C. H. Guenther & Son was promoting its operation as Pioneer Flour Mills, still keeping its corporate name—and the likeness of its founder—on sacks and barrels of Texas Pioneer Flour. The Guenther Milling Company pushed itself as Liberty Mills, reinforcing brand recognition of its Liberty Bell Flour. Under the leadership of Arthur Guenther's successor, Gustav Giesecke, Liberty Mills

By 1904, the scene across the millrace from the 1878 frame mill included, from left, a brick engine house, a three-story brick mill with an addition, a grain elevator and a storage tank.

launched a major expansion, opening a six-story brick and concrete plant in mid-1917. With its adjoining warehouses and elevators, Liberty Mills attained a daily capacity of 800 barrels of flour and 500 barrels of cornmeal, still short of Pioneer's capacity of 1,800 barrels but close enough to keep Pioneer on its toes.

The Guenther family juggernaut at Pioneer also kept its edge in the city's social realm, aided by larger numbers. Arthur and Erhard, who lived at opposite ends of King William Street, kept active in the old German social and fraternal community organizations. Both belonged to the Casino Club. Arthur sang in the Beethoven Mannerchor and was president of the San Antonio Schuetzen Verein, a hunting club. In 1906 Arthur reigned over Carnival Week, the predecessor of San Antonio's Fiesta, as King Selemat II, a designation derived by spelling "tamales" backward.

On the float directly in front of the Alamo in the 1911 Fiesta Battle of Flowers parade is the Queen of Fiesta, Helena Guenther (Muir). In the sedan chair on the next float is the princess, her cousin Regina Beckmann (Hurst).

This calendar plate for 1909, made in Dresden, Germany, marks the first of Pioneer's long-running series of commemorative gift plates at Christmas.

Eight years later Erhard, active in the Beethoven Society and St. John's Lutheran Church, was himself picked for the renamed role of King of Fiesta, an event reigned over on the distaff side in 1911 by two of his nieces, Fritz's daughter Helena as queen and Marie Guenther Beckmann's daughter Regina as princess. Pioneer maintained high visibility during Fiesta Week with its elaborate floats in the annual Trades Parade.

Another annual promotion was launched for 1909 and continued for decades: a series of colorful commemorative plates, most made of the finest china in Dresden, Germany, not far from the ancestral Guenther home. The first types were calendar plates featuring the new year's months around the rim, an allegorical design in the center and, below, the anniversary the mill was marking that year.

In 1912 the U.S. Post Office's newly inaugurated Parcel Post service hit a reported peak in San Antonio business when a Pioneer wagon brought in 900 boxes containing the 1913 souvenir calendar plates being mailed as gifts to customers throughout the state.

In 1909 the Guenther family home still faced the mill and the river as it had when it was built 50 years before.

By this time Erhard Guenther, who at age 23 had skillfully shepherded his parents on their trip to Germany, was becoming a world traveler in his own right. In 1911 he and his wife set off on the first of 18 transoceanic trips, this one an around-the-world voyage. During the trek they purchased numerous items to decorate an expanded home, his parents' modest two-level stone house beside the mill having been enlarged only by a one-story frame addition—in 1880—during a time when the surrounding neighborhood was filling with elaborate homes in the latest styles.

In 1915 the Guenthers transformed the home with an extensive renovation.

The arched entryway facing the home's original orientation toward the mill and river to the south was covered by a three-story addition built of concrete-filled clay tiles reinforced with steel bars and a facade of stone matching that of the original home. On the lower level was a large tea room with porcelain tile floors and stained glass transoms above each window, a 12-foot-high mantelpiece with cast plaster moldings up to the ceiling and light fixtures with alabaster shades over solid cast copper Oriental dragons, their eyes glowing when the fixtures were lit.

As the view from the original front of the Guenther home became increasingly industrial, in 1915 the Erhard Guenthers reoriented the house to the side and rear. The former rear entrance facing Guenther Street, above, remains recognizable in the enlarged home drawn at right, but the main entrance was now from the driveway on the west side.

Erhard and Lottie Guenther brought back ideas and furnishings from their world travels for their renovated home.

On the second floor were two new bedrooms and a bath, on the third a roofed open-air pavilion—later enclosed—with a fireplace for outdoor cooking and an electrically-lit lion's-head fountain. A dumbwaiter in the guise of a wishing well reached down to the first-floor kitchen.

Facing Guenther Street on the north, a dormer over the old part of the house compensated for the new height. A porte cochere on the west replaced the 1880 wing with a main entrance onto the driveway. An oriental note was added to the exterior with ironwork and a green tile roof.

Another factor in Pioneer's growing prosperity was the increasing military presence in South Texas. Not only was the region's sunny climate favorable to uninterrupted military training as World War I approached, the area needed protection from Mexican Revolutionary Pancho Villa, who was making raids across the Rio Grande into Texas and New Mexico.

In mid-1913 Pioneer landed a government contract to supply 67,500 pounds of bran to Fort Clark, 150 miles

To advertise its large contracts with the U.S. Army, Pioneer Flour Mills put signs on the wagons (above) shown on Grayson Street beside Fort Sam Houston's historic Quadrangle as they helped deliver a half-million-pound shipment to the post. Some of the end products were stacked for the promotional photo below. As World War I brought strict rationing of wheat, Pioneer produced Cornserve Flour, shown advertised at right on one of the company's new Packard trucks.

west of the city. The next year Pioneer sent 500,000 pounds of flour across town to Fort Sam Houston's Camp Travis, where a division field bakery was running eight ovens that could turn out 6,000 loaves of bread daily. Soldiers, in turn, were offered tours of the mill. On one occasion, noted Ernst Schuchard in his mill journal, 500 visiting recruits "overran this place like a bunch of wild steers."

With the advent of World War I, Pioneer bought $50,000 in Liberty Bonds, the largest individual purchase in the city. The Army gave Erhard Guenther's wife, Lottie, a ride in a military plane over San Antonio in appreciation for her work with the Red Cross.

As the federal government sought to conserve wheat for the war effort, the nation's mills were urged to shift from milling wheat for civilian use to milling the more plentiful corn crops. "Ours is the splendid burden of feeding the world," the Department of Agriculture trilled to consumers as it explained that there were "at least 50

Growing volumes of paperwork and ledgers were required to keep track of Pioneer's burgeoning business. This view of a corner of the all-male office was snapped in 1914.

By the time of World War I, wooden flour barrels were fully replaced by smaller and more easily handled cloth sacks.

ways" to use cornmeal instead of wheat in preparing meals—for Boston brown bread, dumplings, tamales, croquettes, fish balls.

Persuasion was not just by polite request. Mills were legally prohibited during the war from producing high-grade patent flours and from selling or delivering any wheat flour at all on "wheatless days," Mondays and Wednesdays. To increase use of corn flour, mills were to sell one pound of corn flour for every three of wheat flour. Pioneer responded with a new flour brand, Cornserve.

Meanwhile, C. H. Guenther & Son's expansion program, begun in 1900, continued steadily forward, requiring occasional purchase of adjoining land. Old ways were fading if not altogether disappearing like the wooden flour barrels, finally totally replaced by smaller cloth and paper sacks. Water-powered turbines were converted to generate electricity. Some mule-drawn wagons remained after a fleet of motorized Packard delivery trucks went into use in 1916. An addition to the new brick mill building and another steam engine and boiler added 350 barrels of flour to daily capacity. The grain elevator was enlarged. Four new grain banks added 14,000 bushels of storage capacity.

Location of the mill beside the San Antonio River was a mixed blessing. A flood in 1903 covered mill property with water, as did two more in 1913, when the river rose more than 12 feet and brought water 2 feet deep onto the grounds. Although waterpower no longer drove the grinding machinery, water still flowed through the millrace to turn turbines for auxiliary power.

Space was at a growing premium within the confines of the river bend, though. In 1914 part of the millrace was

This artist's rendering in 1914 conveyed the scope of the Pioneer plant within the river bend, if exaggerating a bit on details. The millrace and train trestle, for example, were enlarged. Behind the new seven-story mill building, the old frame mill, soon to be torn down, was made to look more modern than it was.

spanned by a six-story fireproof mill building of brick, steel and reinforced concrete that upped daily capacity another 600 barrels, to 1,800. Its machinery, the latest manufactured by Milwaukee's Allis-Chalmers Company, used then-innovative ball bearings to reduce friction and increase efficiency. To mitigate destruction from explosions, there were large windows to vent any blast without destroying the entire building, as had happened elsewhere.

The new structure towered briefly above Carl Hilmar Guenther's frame three-story mill, the state of the art in 1878. The old building was then torn down, a victim of the fear of fire and of "the march of progress." A fireproof concrete warehouse later went up on the site, part of a burst of expansion that would mirror the coming prosperity of the 1920s.

Mesquite blocks paved Commerce Street (left) in 1904, when Pioneer Flour Mills set up a promotion series that included the Fiesta Parade, featuring floats with chefs (top left) in 1906 and "pioneers" (top right) in 1922; waffle wagons in parks (above) like one in 1923; and windows displays, as at Fest's Grocery (below) in 1916 at Fredericksburg Road and North Flores Street.

# 6. Prosperity, Depression, Wartime

A battery of six high-rise storage tanks of reinforced concrete, shown on the facing page at the time of their completion in 1929, capped a major Pioneer Flour Mills expansion during the decade. Another major addition was the 20-story square grain elevator, finished in 1922, with crenellations around the top that included mock cannon (above) fashioned out of barrels and pointing to the San Antonio skyline.

Pioneer Flour Mills faced the 1920s with unbridled enthusiasm. Already more grain storage tanks and rail sidings were in place, and planning had begun on a separate office building. Electricity joined water and fuel oil—natural gas would come soon—to power the mills.

In mid-1919 the company took out a line of credit with a New York City bank and began planning an expansion that would nearly double its daily capacity to 3,000 barrels of flour, cornmeal and grain products by 1930. The number of mill workers reached 63—plus 14 office workers—in 1922. Nine years later there were 72, in addition to 21 in the office.

The momentum was sufficient to keep Pioneer profitable through the Depression and to maintain its equilibrium through the shortages of wartime as well.

The centerpiece of the expansion plan was a state-of-the-art grain elevator, a 20-story high-rise square concrete tower amply vented with windows. It received its first rail carload of grain on August 19, 1922. The tower was—and remained for a short time—the tallest structure in the city, and was also reported to be the tallest grain elevator in the South. At the top, signs with "Pioneer" in capital letters on all four sides were lit from 7:30 p.m. to midnight. Since the tower resembled a giant castle turret, in a touch of whimsy crenellations around the rim were interspersed with mock cannon rigged from old wagon wheels and metal columns and drums. For the official unveiling of the structure on October 11, some 250 local grocers and bakers were treated to dinner on the rooftop.

This massive facility prepared the way for the next one. In 1924, after milling engineer Ernst Schuchard and

Several rooftop dinners were hosted at Pioneer Flour Mills beginning in the 1920s. This one, in May 1930 atop the seven-story mill building, feted those attending the 30th annual Texas Bakers Association convention in San Antonio.

Construction had nearly reached the final height on the landmark grain elevator by the end of April 1922.

his head miller, L. T. Darnell, toured mills in St. Louis, St. Joseph and Kansas City, beside the new elevator a seven-story mill building was built of reinforced concrete and brick construction and with an advanced production system of steel rollers.

Then a new engine room was built to house an electrically run steam turbine. The brick mill of 1900 was gutted and refitted as a warehouse, and the old Bates-Corliss steam engine was loaded on a freight car bound for Waelder. Forty tons of old cast iron machinery were sold as scrap.

Storage capacity increased again, in 1929, with a battery of six high-rise reinforced concrete storage tanks next to the elevator. As excavations for the tanks reached ten feet, workmen uncovered fossilized parts of a mastodon's tooth and tusk. Years later, excavators for a truck scale found flint fragments, burned stones and arrowheads at two feet.

By this time, milling technology had reached the point that Pioneer could promote its flour as being made without a human hand ever touching the product, from the time the wheat entered the mill until the sacked flour reached the consumer. Delivered by rail, the raw grain was piped into the elevator, given laboratory tests and, depending on the quality, piped into the appropriate storage tank, all of the tanks "weevil and insect proof."

From there, conveyors carried the grain through cleaning and scouring processes to remove traces of weeds or other foreign matter. Then it was ready to go through the rollers, several types of solid, chilled iron cylinders.

The first rollers were grooved to break the wheat kernels, then sifted through large frames of wire cloth and fine

LEFT: ADOLPH BECKMANN JOURNAL, ERNST SCHUCHARD PAPERS 6/1, DRT LIBRARY

San Antonio's disastrous 1921 flood destroyed the railroad trestle over the river to the mill and caused three weeks of cleanup on the grounds. The city at the time deemed elimination of the bend around the mill too expensive. In 1929 workers, right, began rounding that bend's sharpest tip. Below, the mill's 45-year-old water turbines are removed in 1923 to be replaced and used for continued generation of electricity.

silk gauze to yield a mixture of particles called *middlings*. Larger particles retained by the sifters went to another set of rollers and became bran products. After passing through more rollers and sifters and being purified by a blast of air that carried away any remaining foreign particles, middlings were ground between smooth iron rollers to become—subject to laboratory and kitchen tests—the various brands of flour, machine-dropped into appropriate sacks, sewed shut and sent to warehouses for delivery.

As Pioneer modernized its production process, one time-honored claim fell by the wayside: that, as inscribed even on early commemorative plates, "Pioneer Flour is Pure and Not Bleached." Originally, milled flour had to be

TOP: UT INSTITUTE OF TEXAN CULTURES, COURTESY MRS. FRED STOCKBAUER;
BOTTOM: ERNST SCHUCHARD JOURNAL, ERNST SCHUCHARD PAPERS, DRT LIBRARY

In 1926, flood prevention measures along the San Antonio River south of downtown included blasting away (below) the 1868 dam at the unused Upper Mill, which protruded into the river and was razed. In the process of dredging the river at that point, two millstones were uncovered and placed on the Pioneer grounds. Shown with the stones in about 1935 are four great-granddaughters of Carl Hilmar Guenther, from left: Charlotte Beckmann (Nixon), Dorothy Beckmann (Leslie), Helena Hurst (Harrison) and Anne Schuchard (Hebdon).

stored and physically turned over to age properly and bake the best bread. Small quantities of bleaching agents or additives, however, were found to oxidize the proteins harmlessly just as if the flour had been stored, eliminating the cost and inconsistencies of storage and justifying a lower price. A month after its new elevator opened in 1922, Pioneer began using chlorine gas in a bleaching process.

Despite the increasing reliance on new technology, nature could still vex Pioneer officials. The two old water turbines were being used to power a dynamo to generate electricity in-house for lights and for sewing machines, though when the river was too low—sometimes for months—they could not handle the added strain of lights in the new elevator. Replacement turbines installed in 1923 were also hampered by low river levels.

At the other extreme, a hundred-year flood in September 1921 devastated the central city. Fifty people drowned. Waters also coursed over the riverbanks downstream, wrecking a railroad trestle across the river to the mill and requiring a three-week cleanup on the grounds.

To prevent such disasters in the future, the city accelerated a flood control plan that had already identified the river near the mill as one serious hazard. The easiest blockage to address in the vicinity was the unused dam at the former Upper Mill. It was simply dynamited. Pioneer sought no compensation for its water rights, but asked the city to dredge the river below the old dam and thus increase the water power potential by an equal amount and

BELOW: SAN ANTONIO LIGHT COLLECTION, UT INSTITUTE OF TEXAN CULTURES

A corner inside the Pioneer Flour Mills office building was captured in this snapshot in 1931, as the effects of the Depression were reaching San Antonio.

crease the water power potential by an equal amount downstream.

During the dredging, in 1926, two French burr millstones that had been rolled into the river were uncovered and put on display beside Pioneer's main entrance. The 1868 Upper Mill building—last rented as a garage—extended over the river. The land was sold to the city and the building was razed, though its solid limestone foundations and wheelpit were left in place.

An expensive plan for a cutoff channel to remove the looping bend around the existing mill was scrapped in favor of turning the bend's "V" shape into a "U" and widening the channel from 70 feet up to 150 feet. The project began in late 1929 and was completed the next year. The mill deeded land for the project to the city in exchange for that reclaimed from the old channel.

When the Great Depression hit San Antonio with full force in 1931, Pioneer Flour Mills, in the fortunate niche of providing food essentials, could not be toppled. The cadre of Guenthers working on the inside and those serving on the board of directors had seen that the dramatic expansion of the previous decade did not overextend the com-

In the later Depression years, Pioneer flour sacks were made of ornately printed cloth that could be cut into patterns and resewn as dresses and curtains.

pany's resources, enabling the company even in the darkest years of the 1930s to show a profit and pay dividends to shareholding family members.

Liberty Mills, still the only other flour producer in San Antonio, likewise remained profitable through the Depression, though in the mid-1930s it merged with milling companies in northern Texas, Oklahoma and Kansas and after a decade its San Antonio plant was closed.

In one attempt to rally the economy, the federal government bought wheat directly from farmers to raise the market price, and sold it to mills at the same price. When the market price remained depressed, the government kept buying wheat but paid mills to grind the wheat—for a percentage of the wheat, as in the old barter days of the frontier—and then gave the flour to the Red Cross for free distribution to the needy. It was donated not under the trade names of the mills but as Red Cross Flour. Pioneer ground its first Red Cross Flour in April 1932.

The next year Pioneer signed the National Recovery Act, shortening workers' hours but increasing their pay.

Pioneer also expanded its product line. Varieties of flour, anchored by the Pioneer and White Wings brands

PIONEER FLOUR MILLS 100th ANNIVERSARY ALBUM, ERNST SCHUCHARD PAPERS, DRT LIBRARY

NEWSBOYS' XMAS DINNER, 1936. Guests of E. Guenther.

For two decades Pioneer President Erhard Guenther sponsored a Christmas dinner at the Gunter Hotel for the city's newsboys, who, in return, serenaded Guenther on his birthday. The post-serenade party at Guenther's home, below, occured in 1936.

including Angel Food and Xmas Tree, were augmented with new brands called Mi Amigo and Queen's Crown and with the revival an old brand, Golden Harvest. Packaging was made more convenient for consumers, first by introducing smaller two-pound bags of cloth and less costly paper sacks. Ornately printed flour sacks featured in the later 1930s were recycled by consumers for clothes and curtains.

Super Pioneer Cake Flour and Pioneer Whole Wheat Flour came out in resealable two-and-a half pound canisters. That packaging was also used in Pioneer's expansion into another convenient consumer food product, in the fall of 1932: Breakfast Treat, a cereal mixture of wheat and bran. Sold in one-and-a-half pound canisters, its texture was described by one company official as "about as coarse as corn meal."

A feed mill built in 1937 expanded Pioneer brand offerings for another range of consumers—cows, horses, mules and chickens.

To speed delivery within its core market area, Pioneer in 1936 opened branch warehouses in Austin and Corpus Christi, followed by others in Victoria, Brenham and Wharton. The regional sales force was backed up with heavy promotion.

In addition to prominent product displays in stores were "aerial advertising displays," in which light planes pulled behind them banners touting Pioneer products above cities and towns in many parts of Texas. Such a display was pulled for three hours over Houston one Sunday afternoon in August 1933, followed up, as were the others, with memoranda sent back to San Antonio by dealers and customers certifying that the banners were actually flown.

TOP: PIONEER FLOUR MILLS 100th ANNIVERSARY ALBUM, ERNST SCHUCHARD PAPERS, DRT LIBRARY; BELOW: SAN ANTONIO LIGHT COLLECTION, UT INSTITUTE OF TEXAN CULTURES

For a 1937 Fiesta Trades Parade down Houston Street, Pioneer Flour Mills resurrected the bread basket from a float first used in 1906 and hung from the handle the model of a white wing dove to symbolize White Wings Flour.

When workmen restoring San Antonio's Mission San José uncovered the mission's mill, Ernst Schuchard, Pioneer's milling engineer, helped come up with this reconstruction of the original horizontal millwheel, turned by water pouring from a reservoir above.

Local parades provided another marketing target, from those of Stockdale's Watermelon Festival and the Peanut Festival in Floresville to San Antonio's Fiesta parades—the Trades Parade and parades on the river. In 1940, in the first in the annual series of Fiesta River Parades sponsored by the Texas Cavaliers, Pioneer's Gay Nineties boat helped celebrate completion of the landmark downtown River Walk beautification project. The craft, like others, was strung with lights powered by a truck battery and won third place. In 1939 Pioneer sent a display to the New York World's Fair.

Milling engineer and new corporate secretary Ernst Schuchard, whose strong sense of discipline and introspective bent helped him develop as a skilled artist and draftsman, revealed a playful side in drawings of advertising novelties in his mill journal as he planned company promotions. One cartoon description showed how to make a sign with a face that changes expression—paint one on the front of the glass and another on the back, then change the expression by turning a light on and off behind the glass. Another detailed a display at the Garden Fruit Store down the street featuring a doll that moved as it wrote "Use Pioneer."

    BELOW: PIONEER FLOUR MILLS 100th ANNIVERSARY ALBUM, ERNST SCHUCHARD PAPERS, DRT LIBRARY

A symbolic white wing dove served as the guide for the Pioneer Flour Mills entry in the 1940 River Jubilee parade, the year before completion of the River Walk project. Lights in the lanterns were powered by a truck battery on board as future Pioneer President Alfred Beckmann serenaded his wife, Betty.

He also found that his work with the San Antonio Conservation Society in restoring Mission San José paid promotional dividends.

Schuchard chemically analyzed bits of Spanish paint on the interior of the mission granary's walls so authentic colors could be replicated during the San Antonio Conservation Society's granary's restoration. He did the same sleuthing on the once brightly colored facades of the mission churches at San José and Concepción, and then did definitive watercolors of both.

When workmen in 1935 uncovered an underground room that turned out to be San José's long-lost mission mill, Schuchard analyzed the remains and compared the layout of the site with plans of Spanish mills of the era. He had Pioneer workers replicate the Spanish wooden milling machinery for the rebuilt structure, complete with a horizontal millwheel at the mill's lower level. This project ended up providing the basis for an exhibit on Spanish milling that toured schools in the Rio Grande Valley, accompanied by free booklets on Pioneer's modern operation.

The outbreak of World War II found Pioneer Flour Mills clearing storage areas of unused machinery and coming up

Two breakfast cereals were developed during national emergencies: Breakfast Treat in 1932 during the Depression and Kaffarina in response to corn rationing during World War II.

with a bounty of old equipment to sell for the war effort—some 28 tons of cast iron, 16 tons of steel and 6 tons of mixed iron and steel.

Once again there were government strictures, dealing this time with scarcities less of wheat than of corn. A two-thirds cornmeal cereal marketed in mid-1943 as Kaffarina included one-third wheat flour. Enrichment with such newly popular nutrients as vitamin B, riboflavin, iron and niacin, begun with White Wings Flour in 1941, was expanded to all flours in 1943.

The last Christmas gift plate made in Dresden, Germany in the annual Pioneer Flour Mills series that had begun in 1909 was made in 1939, when relationships were disrupted as war broke out in Europe. For 1942, Pioneer ordered 10,000 Early American–style glass bread plates from the Indiana Glass Company.

As the United States joined the war effort, civilian fuel shortages and gasoline rationing were compounded by a rubber shortage for tires. Pioneer cut its delivery fleet mileage in half by dividing San Antonio into quarters, with one weekly delivery per quarter unless one location ordered a full load.

As had happened during World War I, wartime contracts kept Pioneer running near peak performance. When most of the nation shut down to celebrate Victory in

TOP RIGHT: UT INSTITUTE OF TEXAN CULTURES

Feed production expanded following construction of a new feed mill in 1937.

Europe Day on May 8, 1945, Pioneer Flour Mills remained open to meet the government's production deadline for two railcar loads of flour.

Depression and then wartime created many pent-up demands among American consumers. At Pioneer, these would have to be dealt with by new leadership. On September 25, 1945, Erhard Guenther, 75, died suddenly while having a medical checkup. A week earlier another key executive for the previous 47 years, Sales Manager Arthur Storms, had died at the age of 71.

The time had come for a third generation of Guenthers to move onto center stage.

Pioneer's state of the art milling process in 1925 included roller machines (opposite page) that broke open the kernels, sending wheat flour on through purifiers (top left) and sifters to the packing assembly line—all powered by electric motors (center)—before being stored for rail shipment.

# 7. New Products and New Perils

In one of the numerous anniversary ceremonies during an era of few career changes, Pioneer President Adolph Guenther Beckmann, left, presents a wristwatch to Charlie Metzger, one of four men honored in November 1951 for 40 years of employment. Beckmann himself had already been with his family company for 44 years.

*(Opposite)* Home economist Betty Bradford did a remote radio broadcast—one of Pioneer's numerous regional promotional events of the times—at the 1952 Gillespie County Fair in Fredericksburg.

As the end of World War II redirected America's energies to new opportunities at home, C. H. Guenther & Son Inc.—still preferring to be known as Pioneer Flour Mills—was about to enter its own challenging era.

During its first 94 years, the company had two presidents. In the next 40 years there would be seven. Third- and fourth-generation leaders would be succeeded in turn by chief executives from outside the family, once under tragic circumstances.

Survival for Pioneer Flour Mills would no longer hinge on having reliable waterpower nor on installing the finest grinding equipment, but instead would depend upon the human skills of sensing new directions in time to adapt to the quickly evolving demands of a fast-changing society. And for family milling companies, as for other closely held enterprises, the trend continued ominously toward consolidation and loss of independence. Yet Pioneer continued to defy the odds and stay in charge of its own future.

Its success did not come easily.

The future seemed rosy enough in the fall of 1945, when the mill's presidency passed from Carl Hilmar Guenther's son Erhard to a grandson, Adolph Guenther Beckmann. Beckmann had worked at the mill since his graduation in 1907 from Washington University, where he was captain of the football team. Business was good, and the postwar economic boom was beginning.

But one indisputable sign that new dynamics were at work came in the fall of 1946. Lifting of government-imposed wartime caps on wages led to a nationwide surge of worker demands, and labor unions organized strikes in a host of industries. A Congress of Industrial Organiza-

From the top of Pioneer's grain elevator, burlap sacks laid out to dry after the 1946 flood looked like a sheet of postage stamps.

*A revolution in labor-saving devices in the kitchen after World War II created new demands for convenience in food preparation as well.*

tions drive organizing workers at two San Antonio breweries branched out to include employees at Pioneer Flour Mills as a chapter of the CIO's Food, Tobacco and Agricultural Workers union. More than three-fourths of the mill's 75 production and maintenance employees joined.

Union members at Pioneer soon walked out, shutting down the mill in September 1946 just as one of the century's worst storms sent floodwaters over the San Antonio River's banks and into mill basements, soaking, among other things, a large inventory of burlap sacks. The need to dry out the sacks in particular was not lost on family members in the neighborhood.

"All the cousins came down to the mill," remembers one of Carl Hilmar Guenther's great-grandaughters, Amanda Hurst Ochse, who grew up across the street. She watched a dozen male relatives lug the sacks up from the basement to the ground floor. Others carried the sacks from the ground floor out to the mill lawn, where wives and daughters spread them out. They took three days to dry. From the top of the grain elevator, where he went to take a picture, another great-grandchild, Arthur Muir Jr., remembers that the drying sacks "looked like a sheet of postage stamps."

In less than two weeks the strike was over, as workers and management agreed on a new wage structure.

At the same time, the burgeoning economy was sending the standard of living soaring. Returning soldiers entering the workforce, married and built homes in sprawling subdivisions far from traditional residential neighborhoods. Innovative supermarkets and shopping malls catered to new demands for convenience, as did designers of the suburban homes themselves.

Prime attractions of new homes were the kitchens, filled with the latest labor-saving appliances. Pop-up toasters eliminated the risk for the unwatchful of charred toast in hand-fed toasters. Clothes washers and dryers, even dishwashers, ended regular hours of hand drudgery. Electric refrigerators operated indefinitely at a consistent coolness, without having to be resupplied with blocks of ice like their predecessors. They could store milk, eggs and butter to use whenever it was convenient to prepare food, which at last did not have to be prepared quickly before the newly purchased ingredients spoiled. Stoves came with ovens able to control baking temperatures with a precision previously unknown.

Sparkling kitchens with the latest in labor-saving appliances became standard in new American homes after World War II, when a soaring national economy created a demand for convenience in food preparation.

The culture of convenience embraced convenience in food preparation. Already, wartime powdered food mixes and food drying techniques developed to feed large numbers of troops in the field were being adapted to civilian use. Mixes significantly reduced the number of steps required for flour-based products like biscuits, cakes and pancakes. They could be prepared at a moment's notice using dairy products waiting in refrigerators and spurred a side industry of mixing appliances.

Millers able to see themselves as being less in the milling business than in the food products business adapted to fill the new needs. Adolph Beckmann was one who made the conceptual shift.

Just as Erhard Guenther had revitalized a company long under the management of his predecessor, founder Carl Hilmar Guenther, so did Beckmann inject a burst of innovation following Erhard Guenther's longtime reign. He, too, did it in time to assure the company's survival and future growth. He turned over development of a new product line based on food mixes to his son Alfred.

Work on Pioneer's first food mix, for biscuits, began in earnest in June 1948. The kitchen of the one-story house

Ada Belle Dotson, one of the cooks in Pioneer's new test kitchen, proudly displays an end result of the company's first food mix: hot biscuits.

Pioneer's veteran mill engineer Ernst Fritz Schuchard served as company president from 1954 to 1957.

owned by Pioneer at 127 East Guenther Street, next door to the Guenther House, was turned into a test kitchen. Four white-uniformed women began testing various proportions of dry ingredients. The first boxes of Pioneer Biscuit Mix were produced there six months later. The biscuit mix was so successful that in 1950 a new building was erected specifically for producing prepared mixes.

In November 1950 testing was completed for a pancake mix. Soon chocolate cake mix was being packaged in 18-ounce boxes, joining Pioneer's white cake mix. Cornbread mixes were added as well. The test kitchen moved to the Guenther House after departure of the last residents, Erhard Guenther's daughter Marie Louise Guenther James and her husband, Ted James, Pioneer's vice president.

By the time the company celebrated its centennial in 1951, prepared mixes were well established as the area for major growth. Public demonstrations were held in the Guenther House. Popular home economist Betty Bradford promoted the products on live radio broadcasts in San Antonio and beyond. Five demonstrators were hired for the region's county fairs, club meetings and church gatherings. Hometown appliance stores provided stoves for the demonstrations and gained advertising of their own.

In 1952, Pioneer's mixes were used at the Texas Food Fair in Houston to make a 1,500-pound cake, one of the

TOP: UT INSTITUTE OF TEXAN CULTURES

Once Pioneer Flour Mills brought out its new line of prepared food mixes, food brokers in 1951 quickly picked up on the sales potential.

Addition of a flour tortilla mix helped expand Pioneer's prime marketing area to 12 states.

largest ever baked in the nation. As an incentive to buy Pioneer products, premiums were added with purchases, spawning a variety of future collectibles ranging from metal measuring cups to plastic biscuit cutters to spatulas.

When Adolph Beckmann died in 1954, at the age of 66, the presidency fell to his cousin Ernst Fritz Schuchard, 62, the longtime mill engineer who had worked at the mill since graduating from Stevens Institute of Technology in 1917. Schuchard retired three years later and was succeeded by Pioneer's food mix developer, his predecessor's son Alfred Giles Beckmann, 36, a Texas A&M University graduate and a Bronze Star recipient in World War II.

During Alfred Beckmann's presidency, Pioneer Flour Mills continued to thrive in the continually shrinking field of independent mills, and he served a term as chairman of the Millers' National Federation. Aided by the ongoing growth of food mixes and the addition of a mix for flour tortillas, Pioneer's marketing area expanded to include 12 states, extending west to New Mexico, north to Kansas and east to Tennessee and Alabama.

TOP: UT INSTITUTE OF TEXAN CULTURES

Laddis Kocian holds a box of Pioneer's new Biscuit Mix at the 1949 Fort Bend County Fair in Rosenberg, Texas. A local appliance dealer gained advertising benefits by lending a new electric range to bake sample biscuits. Grocery store promotions included premiums like the aluminum biscuit cutter below.

Administrative needs had long before outgrown the small 1920s office building and spilled into adjoining structures. In 1967 the old office building was razed, as was the old home that had housed the first test kitchen. The two-story brick administrative headquarters that spread over their sites also housed a new quality control laboratory and a finished goods warehouse.

The new building faced Guenther Street and, across it, the new course of the flood-prone San Antonio River. In 1968 the San Antonio River's bend that looped around the mill was shortened in the manner suggested in 1926 and again in 1950. Rather than continuing southwest past the mill on the west as it approached Guenther Street, a new concrete-walled channel turned the river to the southeast, nicking a corner of the Guenther House front lawn and eliminating its side lawn altogether, and also removing Erhard Guenther's old garage.

The new river channel formed a straighter path, eliminating the small peninsula that had provided Carl Hilmar Guenther with his ideal site for a millrace. Filling in the old bend around the mill gave Pioneer new land over which to expand.

Pioneer's food mix innovator Alfred Giles Beckmann, to become company president in five years, stands fourth from the left in this view of the 1,500-pound cake baked with Pioneer Cake Mix at the Texas Food Fair in Houston in 1952.

When Alfred Beckmann resigned in 1973 to accept the presidency of San Antonio's Lone Star Brewing Company, it marked the beginning of the shift to non family management—though not to non family ownership, as the board continued to be made up almost entirely of Guenther family members.

The transition began gently enough with the selection as president of an in-law, Robert Lee Schupbach, 40. Schupbach, Pioneer's sales manager for nearly a decade, was the husband of Erhard Guenther's granddaughter, Helen Guenther James. A Texas A&M University graduate and at first a banker, Schupbach had plans of his own beyond, as could be expected, tightening financial controls.

Soon Schupbach reorganized the thrust of how and where Pioneer's products were sold. Retail sales of Pioneer products by its own force were shifted to a newly formed independent brokerage firm, allowing Pioneer sales repre-

Both the old home (top, right) that once housed Pioneer's first test kitchen and the small 1920s office building behind it were replaced in 1967 with a two-story administrative building and warehouse (below) that connected directly with the main mill building. An entrance to the tile-roofed Guenther House is at the far left in both views.

To move floodwaters more quickly downstream, the U.S. Army Corps of Engineers supervised elimination of the river bend around Pioneer Flour Mills (top left). The river was turned southeast in a walled channel (top right) that replaced the King William and Guenther streets intersection with a bridge and cut through the Guenther House side yard. In January 1968 the new channel reached the bend's return loop (above) as the tophouse of the Tower of the Americas in the distance was on its way up just in time for the opening three months later of HemisFair '68, the world's fair that reenergized the city.

sentatives to target a new market—the food service and restaurant industry, which welcomed the convenience of food mixes. Working with quality control personnel, Schupbach spearheaded development of a gravy mix to augment these sales. Revenue moved sharply upward.

Robert Schupbach, diagnosed with emphysema, was able to have his successors in place by the time of his death in January 1982 at the age of 48. Chairmanship of the board, previously held by the company's president, was made an independent position. That went to Scott Petty Jr., 45, a fellow in-law whose wife, the former Louise James, and Schupbach's wife were sisters. Petty, a University of Texas engineering graduate and rancher, had been president of his family's geophysical engineering business while also serving on Pioneer's board.

Promoted to president was F. Michael Wood, 36, the chief financial officer, who had been with Pioneer since 1975 and who became the first president with no Guenther family ties. Wood had worked closely with Schupbach in developing and marketing the new gravy mix.

Although the food service thrust had spread to 42 states, retail sales in Pioneer's 12-state core area were falling behind—despite the success of Pioneer's White Wings Flour Tortilla Mix, outselling all competing mixes combined by four to one. Wood set out to strengthen research and development of new products.

Wood had hardly settled into his job when in May 1982, five months after he took office, the small plane in

Despite the deaths of two presidents of C. H. Guenther & Son in less than six months, descendants of Carl Hilmar and Dorothea Guenther, many of them shown above at a gathering with their spouses in 1972, determined to maintain family ownership of the company.

Robert Schupbach, Pioneer's president since 1973, was focusing on development of a new convenience food product line at the time of his death in 1982 at the age of 48.

which he was returning from a fishing trip in Mexico crashed some 50 miles southwest of San Antonio. All seven persons aboard were killed.

"I was asked to go on that trip," Petty remembered. "But I decided to tend to some things here. Before he left, Mike insisted on showing me how he had organized the files and where he put things. If he hadn't, we'd have had an even more difficult transition than we did."

In an emergency board meeting the day after the plane crash, Board Chairman Scott Petty was made Wood's successor. "The board was adamant about not selling the company or even entertaining some of the offers that started coming in," Petty recalled. "The board members were determined to take the time to make the company into something greater."

The pressure on Petty was intense. Not only had the 200-employee Pioneer Flour Mills lost its president of ten years a few months earlier and now the longtime executive who had just succeeded him, but a third veteran executive was about to retire after a career of 45 years. That was Vice President for Purchasing Brentano Harnisch, a nephew of Lottie Guenther Harnisch and, other than Petty, the last person then in management connected to the Guenther family.

Petty's first goal was to reestablish a management team and replace himself as chief executive officer.

Michael Wood, 36, Pioneer's first president with no ties to the Guenther family, (top) was killed in a plane crash after five months in office. Board Chairman Scott Petty Jr. (center) assumed the presidency until former Beatrice Foods executive Richard DeGregorio (below) was chosen in 1984.

During an extensive national search, one name for the top post kept surfacing: that of Richard R. DeGregorio, head of a special products division in Covington, Ohio for Beatrice Foods, one of the nation's leading food companies and a supplier to Pioneer. A Chicago native and Loyola University of Chicago graduate with a Northwestern University master's degree in business administration, DeGregorio was a veteran of the national food industry's corporate scene with just the mix of chemistry, technology and management background that Petty was looking for.

Within months DeGregorio was in San Antonio, starting out as Pioneer's executive vice president for sales, marketing and operations. Brought in as vice president for planning was Bill Cothren, previously president of a San Antonio–based food products transportation company. Including Petty, the fourth top manager became Mary Hitt, a Pioneer veteran of ten years in accounting and finance, who was named secretary-treasurer.

With the same sort of enthusiasm that more than a century earlier another trained and experienced miller, Carl Hilmar Guenther, had brought from afar to the South Texas milling industry, Richard DeGregorio took aim as soon as he reached San Antonio at what he saw as a wealth of opportunities on a new frontier.

But first, some questions needed to be answered.

Did people like what Pioneer produced? Marketing research in San Antonio, the Rio Grande Valley, New Orleans and Memphis confirmed satisfaction with Pioneer products.

Also, who were Pioneer's potential customers, and just why were so many of them buying General Mills products, leaving Pioneer's market share in second place in its own 12-state core region?

Most potential buyers, it turned out, were in the nation's fastest-growing region, the South. Many were between the ages of 24 to 49, had small families and were often new arrivals, and so brought with them old buying patterns. They most likely had not heard of Pioneer.

Outdated package graphics were made more contemporary with warm blue and orange tones. Glossy color photos of the finished product went on the boxes along with more recipe ideas to broaden product use—like how to make crepes with pancake mix, sopapillas with French donut mix and hush puppies with cornbread mix. Package sizes were reduced to accommodate the younger, smaller

With Pioneer Flour Mills able to expand beyond the small peninsula once formed by the now-rerouted San Antonio River, the warehouse in the foreground could be constructed in the early 1980s over reclaimed land.

families who only needed smaller portions. A new slogan blended the regional approach with the appeal of tradition: "Southern Success Since 1851."

With those changes in place, in September 1983 Pioneer launched its first major television advertising campaign, targeting the 24- to 49-year-old age group. The 30-week holiday baking season blitz spread from Texas and New Mexico east to Georgia.

As sales took an unprecedented rise and Pioneer's market share crept upward, the manufacturing plant itself was readied for more growth. Adjacent land facing South Main Avenue, accessible across the now-filled-in river channel, was purchased for expansion. The laboratory was divided into quality control and research development departments and given new space. A 55,000-square-foot warehouse was built on land reclaimed from the old riverbed. White Wings Corn Tortilla Mix joined Pioneer's long-popular mix for flour tortillas.

His apprenticeship a resounding success, in 1984—two years after his arrival—Richard DeGregorio became Pioneer's ninth president and chief executive officer. Scott Petty Jr., with some relief, moved back to being chairman of the board. Bill Cothren gained the title of executive vice president and chief operating officer.

Soon came another marketing breakthrough.

Southerners traditionally enjoy gravy on their biscuits. In 1985 Pioneer came out with its long-planned Old Fash-

During new work on the river in 1981, a steel coffer dam blocks water from the old wheelbay of Guenther's 1868 Upper Mill while original timbers are removed for preservation and numbered foundation stones are lifted out, to be replaced on a new footing and be ready for some future reconstruction of the mill.

BOTH: UTSA CENTER FOR ARCHAEOLOGY RESEARCH

ioned Country Gravy Mix for the retail market. The gravy mixes were eventually expanded into 12 varieties, from chicken to turkey to roasted garlic to three non fat mixes. They became the company's top-selling product line.

While Pioneer Flour Mills was taking to the air waves and expanding its sales in distant states, the company was not overlooking opportunities in its own—literally—backyard, nor forgetting where it came from.

One dramatic reminder of Pioneer's origins came in 1981 during planning for widening and deepening the San Antonio River channel south of downtown. In compliance with federal requirements, the U.S. Army Corps of Engineers hired the Center for Archaeological Research at the University of Texas at San Antonio to excavate and study remains of the 1868 Upper Mill prior to clearing some of the site. Although the building had been removed during a flood control project in 1926, foundations and rubble from the millwheel pit remained an obstruction in the channel.

A corrugated steel diversion wall was built around the site, and standing water within was pumped out. Then an archeological research team led by Anne Fox and a construction crew with bulldozer and backhoe began 16 days of work. First they removed and documented stone foundations from the former wheelpit and its forebay. The

The gilt-framed mirror in the parlor of the Carl Hilmar Guenther home, built beside the mill in 1859 and enlarged in 1915, reflects a workman in the process of restoring the landmark structure into the Guenther House, above, a combination restaurant, banquet facility, museum and retail outlet that opened to the public in 1988.

original floor of cypress timbers was taken up and stored to assure its preservation.

Stones from the mill's riverside wall were removed, numbered and reassembled atop a new concrete foundation extending 32 inches farther down to the new lower level of the channel. In the process, workmen turned up an apparent mate to the original French burr millstone found during dredging of the river 55 years before.

In their 108-page report the archeologists concluded, "Guenther was a careful builder who followed the basic precepts of good mill construction."

While reconstruction of the Upper Mill's foundations was done carefully to stabilize them for some eventual rebuilding of the mill, another historic preservation project was about to yield immediate final results, this one at the still-flourishing site of the Lower Mill: restoration of the Guenther home.

Built by the founder when he came to San Antonio in 1859 and enlarged and transformed to three stories by a son in 1915, the structure was last used as a family home in the late 1940s, when it was converted in part to a test kitchen and then used for offices or storage. The decision to restore it came in 1986.

Working with such authenticity that the home was later approved for listing on the National Register of His-

The tile floored family room, with its stained glass window panels and mantel with motifs of wheat and corn, now serves as the main dining area in the Guenther House.

toric Places, the parlor was refurbished as a museum room with its original furniture and family paintings. Bookcases in the adjoining library were filled with Pioneer memorabilia, from Dresden souvenir plates to Guenther family schoolbooks to cookie cutters.

On the lower level, the dining room and the large tile-floored family room with its Art Nouveau stained glass window panels and decorative plaster became a restaurant, spilling outdoors to the adjoining arbor. The main bedroom and the former music room became the River Mill Store, offering Pioneer products and gift items and supporting a new mail-order catalog business. The old roof garden, with its open terrace, was restored for private meetings and dinners.

By the time the Guenther House opened to the public in March 1988, company officials were in the midst of pursuing a new, far-reaching strategy for overall corporate growth.

# 8. Beckoning Horizons

In the mid-1980s Pioneer Flour Mills had some hard choices to face.

To continue business as usual—marketing Pioneer's traditional products of flour, corn meal and prepared mixes within its six-state core area—would leave the company's market share vulnerable to the ongoing national advertising onslaughts of food company giants.

It would be dangerously expensive, though, for Pioneer to attempt to enlarge its primary marketing area. Outside lay other strong regional companies aggressively defending their turf plus the larger food manufacturers, exploiting even within Pioneer's own region the fastest-growing segment of the food industry: frozen foods, which required no mixing but simply had to be thawed. Their manufacture required equipment and expertise well beyond Pioneer's capability.

Yet Pioneer Flour Mills, as C. H. Guenther & Son Inc. continued to be known, considered itself no sleepy provincial enterprise content to plod along with little thought of any need to change. The company's post–World War II thrust may have been slowed by the premature deaths of two presidents, but its new management team—with strong credentials in the food industry—had reexamined and repositioned operations to the point that Pioneer could take on new challenges, whatever they happened to be.

The first break came in 1987, when Pioneer was successful in targeting Texas Custom Bakers Inc., 200 miles to the north in the Dallas suburb of Duncanville, for acquisition. Texas Custom Bakers had been established in 1968 as one of Hart's Bakery's three regional plants making frozen

*(Opposite)* The main grain elevator and battery of storage tanks at Pioneer Flour Mills are mirrored in the mid-1980s in the waters of the redirected San Antonio River, as company executives themselves were reflecting on repositioning the company within the food industry.

*(OPPOSITE) SAN ANTONIO EXPRESS-NEWS* COLLECTION, UT INSTITUTE OF TEXAN CULTURES

Pioneer Flour Mills went into the frozen foods business with the acquisition in 1987 of its first subsidiary, Texas Custom Bakers in the Dallas suburb of Duncanville. The name was changed to Wheatland Farms and then to Pioneer Frozen Foods.

pull-apart yeast rolls, and soon it added other frozen foods. The company, under private ownership since 1982 following several interim owners, had just added a new product—frozen baked biscuits. That was a logical extension of Pioneer's line.

"Buying that company was a risk," reflected Pioneer President Richard DeGregorio. "But it was a greater risk not to buy it."

The transition of Texas Custom Bakers to Pioneer ownership was not easy, with employee turnover and difficult operational adjustments. "Sometimes I thought it would mean the end of my time as chairman of the board," Scott Petty Jr.—who is still chairman—could laugh later. The subidiary's name was changed to Wheatland Farms, and then, seven years later, to Pioneer Frozen Foods.

By the early 1990s, Pioneer Flour Mills had regained its stride. There had been a major physical expansion at the frozen food division, which was functioning as originally planned. New types of profitable gravy mixes were coming out with a seemingly effortless regularity. Pioneer became the first in-plant manufacturer of a convenient non round resealable and reusable canister for biscuit and baking mixes. In 1993 the company completed implementation and training for a rigorous planning system that pointed the way to meeting market demands of the future.

Pioneer was even expanding its market in northern Mexico by exporting a dozen additional products into af-

In a network design worthy of interstate highway engineers, conveyors at Pioneer Frozen Foods in suburban Dallas help move frozen biscuits.

In 1993 Pioneer Flour Mills became the first food company to manufacure in house a non-round, resealable and reusable biscuit and baking mix container.

fluent areas where Pioneer's White Wings Flour Tortilla Mix had traditionally done well. Demographic trends pointed the way to expansion in the upper midwestern United States, where immigrants with roots in northern Mexico took with them their brand preference for White Wings Flour Tortilla Mix and the wheat-based flour tortillas that region prefers over the more broadly favored corn tortillas.

Pioneer Flour Mills was ready for another step.

Soon word spread in the food industry that a somewhat smaller counterpart to Pioneer Flour Mills—The White Lily Foods Company of Knoxville, Tennessee—was for sale. Despite having had four owners in the previous two decades, White Lily's management remained stable and maintained high-quality production of White Lily Flour, such a southeastern regional food icon that it appeared on kitchen shelves in the Academy Award–winning film "Driving Miss Daisy."

Pioneer officials saw the fit.

Pioneer's Southern Success pitch was already boosting sales eastward into Alabama, the western edge of the White Lily marketing area that continued north into Kentucky and east and south to Virginia and Florida. The Knoxville company, like Pioneer, had a line of prepared mixes for biscuits, pancakes, cornbread and muffins and was likewise a major supplier to restaurants in its region. But Pioneer Flour, made with hard wheat ideal for bread and tortillas, lacked the fine soft wheat texture of White Lily Flour, so beloved for southern biscuits. Supply and storage aside, logistics for adding the special milling equipment for soft wheat in San Antonio were daunting.

The White Lily Food Company, acquired in 1995, was established in Knoxville, Tennessee, in 1882 by entrepreneur James Allen Smith, and by 1896 was producing White Lily Flour.

For decades, Pioneer Flour Mills had prided itself in having no long-term debt. Except for Carl Hilmar Guenther's loans from his father and fellow townsmen in the earliest days, the company had taken on major financial obligations only for the expansion of the San Antonio mill that began in 1919. But Board Chairman Scott Petty and President Richard DeGregorio made a convincing case to Guenther's descendants on the board. After three months of consideration, on January 13, 1995, C. H. Guenther & Son Inc. closed on the financing and purchased The White Lily Foods Company.

Similarities between the two companies were indeed striking. White Lily was also a major industry in a regional commercial center—Knoxville, a city of 165,000 people nestled in a river valley in the mountains of eastern Tennesee. White Lily, too, had grown to regional dominance under majority ownership of the family of its founder, also a relatively young outsider with an ingrained work ethic. And much of its success was similarly attributed to a company culture that, starting with the founder, emphasized quality products.

White Lily had emerged as a brand name by 1896, around the time Carl Hilmar Guenther and other millers

Acquisition of the prestigious White Lily brand products in 1995 also added the southeastern United States to the Pioneer and White Wings brands primary distribution area.

throughout America began putting appealing names on specific products. White Lily was the creation of Georgia-born Knoxville entrepreneur James Allen Smith. In 1882 Smith gathered some local investors to establish a fast-growing milling operation, incorporated in 1883 and soon known as J. Allen Smith and Company.

As in Texas, the regional market responded to Smith's insistence on high-quality products. Sales expanded to neighboring states. White Lily maintained a family flour market share of at least 75 percent in Knoxville and 53 percent in Atlanta.

When Powell Smith retired as the company's president in 1939, 19 years after his father's death, company leadership first fell to Frank Tucker, who picked up on the

Now having a trio of widely-known brands—Pioneer, White Wings and White Lily— in 1999 Pioneer Flour Mills went back to using its official corporate name: C. H. Guenther & Son, Inc. Officiating at designation ceremonies are Board Chairman Scott Petty Jr., far left, and President Richard DeGregorio, far right, assisted by rancher Hilmar Guenther Moore, a great-grandson of Carl Hilmar Guenther.

postwar trend toward streamlined production and convenience foods, and then to Leo Driscoll and James Skidmore. In 1963 the Smiths sold their remaining stock.

But Knoxville management, perhaps against the odds, remained sufficiently stable through a succession of conglomerate ownerships to maintain White Lily's quality standards. Under the local leadership of Willard Toevs, and after 1979 under Ted Pedas, White Lily was owned by some of the nation's largest food companies—Great Western United, Federal Company, Tyson Foods and then Archer Daniels Midland, which in 1989 sold the company to Windmill Corporation, the venture capital group that sold it to C. H. Guenther & Son.

Ted Pedas retired as White Lily president and was succeeded by Pioneer's Richard DeGregorio, who remained chief executive of the San Antonio mill as well as of Pioneer Frozen Foods in suburban Dallas.

With the acquisition of The White Lily Foods Company and its deeply rooted milling heritage in the Southeast, Pioneer's products were on store shelves in 28 states, extending as far north as Ohio and Illinois.

Of the 50 consumer products, White Wings and Pioneer brand products made up half, Pioneer Cajun Brown and Jalapeño Country gravy mixes being the latest additions. The others were White Lily brand products, from self-rising flour and cornmeal to Blueberry Pancake, Apple Cinnamon Muffin and Chewy Fudge Brownie mixes. All were in addition to generic products and products custom-made for a host of restaurant and institutional clients.

These top-selling consumer products of C. H. Guenther & Son, Inc. are marketed throughout much of the nation under three brand names: Pioneer, White Wings and White Lily. Many other products are made in bulk according to the specifications of a variety of institutions and restaurant companies.

Pioneer, White Wings and White Lily brands were granted parity in 1999 as a well-publicized promotion replaced the familiar name of Pioneer Flour Mills with the corporate umbrella name: C. H. Guenther & Son Inc., the parent company's legal if seldom-used corporate designation for the previous century.

By its 150th anniversary year of 2001, C. H. Guenther & Son, Inc. had become what is believed to be not only the oldest family-owned business in Texas, but also the oldest continuously-operated family-owned milling company in the United States. C. H. Guenther & Son was using nearly 10 million bushels of wheat and corn each year for nearly 100 products and employing some 725 persons—425 in San Antonio, 150 in suburban Dallas at Pioneer Frozen Foods and 150 at the White Lily plant in Knoxville.

Of the company's 100 shareholders, more than 90 remained descendants of Carl Hilmar Guenther and were committed, according to Board Chairman Scott Petty, to the company's continued independence.

As for future directions, President Richard DeGregorio could point to the goal summary of the five-year strategic plan charged to a young management team led by former Quaker Oats executive Dale Tremblay, executive vice president and chief operating officer: "Be a leading supplier of gravies and sauces, baking mixes and other value-added, grain-based food products to the food service industry and selected consumer markets in North America."

Yesterday, Texas. Today, the South and the Midwest. Tomorrow, North America?

Well, in the can-do spirit of Carl Hilmar Guenther, why not?

C. H. Guenther & Son's food products now extend beyond flour to frozen foods and mixes for a variety of foods, from gravies to biscuits to pancakes to tortillas.

C. H. Guenther & Son's main plant in San Antonio is still distinguished by its 20-story grain elevator, built in 1922.

In 1855 Hermann Lungkwitz painted *Guenther's Mill on Live Oak Creek* by Guenther's first home, near Fredericksburg.

Robert J. Onderdonk painted Guenther's 1868 Upper Mill after its waterwheel was replaced with a water turbine.

BELOW: WITTE MUSEUM, SAN ANTONIO, TEXAS

Built in 1859 by Carl Hilmar
Guenther, enlarged in 1915 by his
son Erhard and restored in 1988, the
Guenther House is a major visitor
destination in San Antonio as a
combination museum, restaurant,
banquet site and gift store. During
the Christmas season, the spirit of
the family's early gatherings is
captured in the restored parlor, and
lighted reindeer are poised on the
side lawn. Tables in the roof garden
are set for a special dinner, while
the River Mill Store features gift
items and food products related to
cooking and baking.

In 1899, C. H. Guenther & Son, just incorporated, reorganized its product line with names for twelve new brands. The two flours receiving the heaviest promotion were Pioneer, featuring the likeness of the company's founder, and White Wings, named for the region's white wing doves. These designs were used on the brands' barrelheads until wooden barrels were discontinued about 1920.

Pioneer Flour Mills was promoting unbleached flour when this broadside was printed in 1907.

This cardboard figure carried an actual miniature flour sack.

In 1915, encouragement to buy local products was aimed at housewives, "the power behind the household."

Commemorative plates made in Dresden, Germany from 1909 until the beginning of World War II were used by Pioneer Flour Mills as Christmas gifts. These calendar plates reflect a shift in Pioneer's manufacturing methods. In 1922 the mill began the efficient bleaching process for its milled flour, resulting in a change in its slogan from Pioneer Flour as being "Pure and Not Bleached" to being simply "Pure and Nutritious."

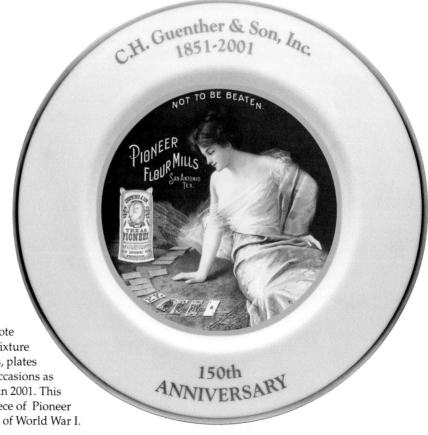

In addition to distributing plates, in 1933 Pioneer Flour Mills gave a Dresden cereal bowl to help promote its new Breakfast Treat, a boxed mixture of wheat and bran. Since the 1940s, plates have been made on such special occasions as the company's 150th anniversary, in 2001. This plate made by Lenox features a piece of Pioneer advertising art designed in the era of World War I.

# Chronology

1851— Carl Hilmar Guenther, 24, an immigrant from Germany, builds a flour mill near Fredericksburg, Texas after a journey of nearly three years through New York, Wisconsin and Louisiana.

1852— Floodwaters destroy Guenther's mill dam, causing him to go more deeply in debt as he rebuilds.

1855— His mill profitable, Guenther replaces his log home with a larger one of rock and marries Dorothea Pape, daughter of neighboring German immigrants.

1856— Guenther expands the mill with an additional waterwheel and two more millstones from France, though a long-term drought begins reducing wheat crops.

1859— Threatened by a new steam mill in Fredericksburg, Guenther sells his mill to his father-in-law. Aided by an inheritance from Germany, he buys a site in the more promising town of San Antonio and builds a home nearby.

1860— Guenther completes his new mill on the San Antonio River.

1865— Guenther survives the Civil War after supplying flour to the Confederacy and banking his funds in Germany.

1868— Capacity increases with construction of a second mill just upstream. The C. H. Guenther family is complete with the birth of a seventh child, their fourth son.

1875— Guenther's Best becomes the brand name for the top grade of flour.

1877— Guenther replaces his original San Antonio mill with a larger building as construction of a railroad to San Antonio expands his ability to ship flour out, though also outside competitors' ability to ship flour in.

1878— Guenther Mills becomes C. H. Guenther & Sons, as Fritz, 21, and Arthur, 19, join their father in a partnership.

1888— C. H. Guenther & Sons win four first premiums for quality at the San Antonio International Exposition.

1892— Steel rollers begin replacing millstones to grind grain, allowing greater control and increasing production. Other new technology soon to be implemented includes steam power and the latest sifting equipment.

1894— C. H. Guenther & Sons becomes C. H. Guenther & Son, as Arthur Guenther leaves to join relatives of his wife in a competing company known as Liberty Mills and then also as The Guenther Milling Company. During its some 50 years of existence the new mill never overtakes the older company.

1898— Following the death of eldest son Fritz, C. H. Guenther & Son incorporates under the management of youngest son Erhard, 30.

1899— During a brand name disagreement with the breakaway son's Guenther Milling Company, C. H. Guenther & Son trademarks 12 new flour brands, among them Texas Pioneer, bearing the likeness of founder C. H. Guenther, and White Wings.

1900— A three-story steam-powered mill is added on the original San Antonio River site to replace production of the upstream 1868 mill, closed and rented with its water power to a manufacturer of macaroni.

1902— Founder Carl Hilmar Guenther dies at the age of 76.

1909— C. H. Guenther & Son, at this point preferring to be known as Pioneer Flour Mills after its most popular brand, begins an annual series of commemorative gift plates.

1914— A six-story building of steel and concrete is built to replace the 1877 frame mill building and to increase production, helping fill new orders from San Antonio's growing military establishment.

**1915**— Mill President Erhard Guenther transforms his parents' modest home beside the mill into a three-story landmark with oriental motifs.

**1916**— Motorized Packard delivery trucks begin replacing mule-drawn wagons. Delivery also soon becomes easier with replacement of wooden flour barrels by smaller and lighter cloth and paper sacks.

**1918**— World War I food conservation requirements lead to production of Cornserve Flour, ground from corn rather than wheat.

**1919**— New York financing is secured to begin doubling Pioneer's production capacity over the next ten years.

**1922**— A 20-story concrete grain elevator, for a short time the tallest structure in the city, is completed.

**1924**— Additional construction is highlighted by a seven story mill building of reinforced concrete.

**1926**— Start of flood prevention work on the San Antonio River south of downtown includes removal of the unused 1868 mill building upstream and its dam.

**1929**— Six concrete storage tanks cap company expansion.

**1932**— Introduction of Breakfast Treat wheat cereal marks Pioneer's entry into consumer convenience foods. Depression-fighting techniques include Red Cross Flour made from government-owned wheat and cloth flour sacks designed for recycling into clothes and curtains.

**1936**— Promotion to maintain market strength is accompanied by new branch warehouses in Austin and Corpus Christi, followed by ones in Victoria, Brenham and Wharton. Spanish mill restoration at San José Mission includes wooden equipment designed by Pioneer's mill engineer Ernst Schuchard.

**1937**— A new feed mill expands products for farm animals.

**1940**— Pioneer has a prize-winning entry in the first Texas Cavaliers Fiesta River Parade, dedicating the new San Antonio River Walk.

**1943**— Wartime food regulations lead to production of Kaffarina cereal, reducing wheat use by being two-thirds cornmeal. Vitamin enrichment is expanded to all flours.

**1945**— Pioneer President Erhard Guenther dies at 75 and is succeeded by a nephew, Adolph Guenther Beckmann.

**1948**— Six months of work in a test kitchen leads to marketing of Pioneer Biscuit Mix, developed under Adolph Beckmann's son Alfred.

**1950**— Biscuit mix success leads to a new building for prepared mixes, soon including cake, pancake and cornmeal mixes.

**1951**— Pioneer celebrates its centennial.

**1952**— Promotion of mixes includes participation in regional fairs and parades and baking a 1,500-pound cake with Pioneer Cake Mix at the Texas Food Fair in Houston.

**1954**— Pioneer President Adolph Beckmann dies at 66 and is succeeded by his cousin Ernst Schuchard, 60.

**1957**— Ernst Schuchard retires as president and is succeeded by Alfred Beckmann.

**1967**— New office building and warehouse added to help serve a 12-state marketing area west to New Mexico, east to Tennessee and Alabama, north to Kansas and south into northern Mexico.

**1968**— In a flood control measure the San Antonio River, which looped around Pioneer Flour Mills to the west, is rerouted in a new channel around the opposite side to the east.

**1972**— White Wings Flour Tortilla Mix is introduced and becomes a fast-selling product

**1973**— Alfred Beckmann resigns as president and is succeeded by Robert Schupbach, vice president of sales. Marketing begins to the food service and restaurant industry.

**1981**— Flood control work on San Antonio River channel includes archeological excavation of C. H. Guenther's 1868 mill site upstream.

**1982**— Robert Schupbach dies at 48 and is succeeded by Michael Wood, 36, chief financial officer. Five months later Wood is killed in a plane crash and is succeeded by Board Chairman Scott Petty Jr.

**1983**— Pioneer launches its "Southern Success Since 1851" regional advertising campaign.

**1984**— Scott Petty Jr. reverts to board chairman and is succeeded as president by Richard DeGregorio. Major warehouse, new quality control and research development laboratories are built.

**1985**— Flour-based Old-Fashioned Country Gravy Mix—first in a line of gravy mixes—is introduced and soon becomes company's best-selling product.

**1987**— Acquisition of Texas Custom Bakers in suburban Dallas puts Pioneer in the frozen baked goods and biscuits market. Subsidiary is renamed Wheatland Farms and, later, Pioneer Frozen Foods.

**1988**— After a two-year restoration of the C. H. Guenther home, begun beside the mill in 1859, the Guenther House opens as a restaurant with retail sales and historical exhibits.

**1991**— Texas Taco and Chili Seasoning mixes are introduced.

**1992**— No-Fat Biscuit and Baking Mix becomes Pioneer's most successful launch of a new product.

**1993**— Pioneer becomes the world's first manufacturer of a convenient nonround, resealable and reusable canister for baking and biscuit mixes.

**1995**— The White Lily Foods Company of Knoxville, Tennessee, longtime manufacturers of White Lily Flour and numerous other brands, is acquired, expanding Pioneer's marketing area throughout the Southeast.

**1996**— White Wings Ready-to-Eat Flour Tortillas is introduced.

**1999**— Corporate identity, long under the Pioneer Flour Mills name, is reasserted as C. H. Guenther & Son, Inc., the legal designation since 1898. Plants in San Antonio, suburban Dallas and Knoxville have 725 employees, and products approaching national distribution.

**2001**— The sesquicentennial year of C. H. Guenther & Son, Inc.

# Bibliography

Burkholder, Mary V. *The King William Area: A History and Guide to the Houses.* San Antonio: King William Association, 1973.

Chabot, Frederick C. *With the Makers of San Antonio.* San Antonio: Artes Graficas, 1937.

Davis, Sharon P., ed. *From Wheat to Flour.* Washington and Englewood, Colorado: Millers' National Federation and Wheat Foods Council, 1996.

Everett, Donald E. *San Antonio: The Flavor of Its Past.* San Antonio: Trinity University Press, 1975.

Fisher, Lewis F. *Crown Jewel of Texas: The Story of San Antonio's River.* San Antonio: Maverick Publishing Company, 1997.

_____. *Saving San Antonio: The Precarious Preservation of a Heritage.* Lubbock: Texas Tech University Press, 1996.

Fox, Anne A., and Lois M. Flynn and I. Waynne Cox. *Archaeological Studies for the San Antonio Channel Improvement Project, Including Investigations at Guenther's Upper Mill (41BX 342).* San Antonio: Archaeological Survey Report No. 136, Center for Archaeological Research, The University of Texas at San Antonio, 1987.

Guenther, Carl Hilmar. Translated by Regina Beckmann Hurst, introduction by Walter D. Kamphoefner. *An Immigrant Miller Picks Texas: The Letters of Carl Hilmar Guenther.* San Antonio: Maverick Publishing Company, 2001.

Hamilton, Neil A. "J. Allen Smith and White Lily Foods: Speculums of Modern America," 1982. Manuscript prepared for abridged publication in *Journal of East Tennessee History*, photocopy in C. H. Guenther & Son, Inc. archives, San Antonio, Texas.

Jackson, A. T. *Mills of Yesteryear.* El Paso: Texas Western Press, The University of Texas at El Paso, 1971.

Kamphoefner, Walter D., and Wolfgang Helbich and Ulrike Sommers, eds. *News from the Land of Freedom: German Immigrants Write Home.* Ithaca: Cornell University Press, 1991.

Kuhlmann, Charles Byron. *The Development of the Flour-Milling Industry in the United States.* Boston and New York: Houghton Mifflin Company, 1929.

McGuire, James Patrick. *Hermann Lungkwitz: Romantic Landscapist on the Texas Frontier.* Austin: The University of Texas Press for The University of Texas Institute of Texan Cultures at San Antonio, 1983.

[Pfeiffer], Ann Maria Watson. "National Register of Historic Places Registration Form, Carl Hilmar Guenther House," 1989. San Antonio Conservation Society Library, San Antonio, Texas. Photocopy.

Schuchard, Ernst. Papers. The Daughters of the Republic of Texas Library at the Alamo, San Antonio, Texas.

[Schuchard, Ernst, ed.]. *100th Anniversary Pioneer Flour Mills, San Antonio, Texas, 1851–1951.* San Antonio: The Naylor Company, 1951.

Steinfeldt, Cecilia. *San Antonio Was: Seen Through a Magic Lantern.* San Antonio: The San Antonio Museum Association, 1978.

# Index